THE 100-YARD CLASSROOM

Also from the Boys Town Press

The Well-Managed Classroom
Tools for Teaching Social Skills in School
Teaching Social Skills to Youth
No Room for Bullies
Safe and Effective Secondary Schools
Changing Children's Behavior by Changing
    the People, Places, and Activities in Their Lives
Treating Youth with DSM-IV Disorders
Getting Along with Others
Common Sense Parenting
There Are No Simple Rules for Dating My Daughter
Who's Raising Your Child?
Angry Kids, Frustrated Parents
Common Sense Parenting of Toddlers and Preschoolers
Unmasking Sexual Con Games
Good Night, Sweet Dreams, I Love You:
    Now Get into Bed and Go to Sleep
Parenting to Build Character in Your Teen
Practical Tools for Foster Parents
Skills for Families, Skills for Life

For Adolescents
Guys, Let's Keep It Real
Little Sisters, Listen Up
Boundaries: A Guide for Teens
A Good Friend
Who's in the Mirror?
What's Right for Me?

For a free Boys Town Press catalog, call 1-800-282-6657
or visit our website: www.boystownpress.org

Girls and Boys Town National Hotline 1-800-448-3000
Parents and kids can call toll-free, anytime, with any problem

THE 100-YARD CLASSROOM

Winning Strategies for Helping Kids Succeed in School, Sports, and Life

by
Kevin Kush, M.A.

BOYS TOWN, NEBRASKA

THE 100-YARD CLASSROOM

Published by the Boys Town Press
Father Flanagan's Boys' Home
Boys Town, Nebraska 68010

Girls *and* Boys Town

HELP · HEALING · HOPE

The Boys Town Press is the publishing division of Girls and Boys Town, the original Father Flanagan's Boys' Home.

Publisher's Cataloging in Publication Data

Kush, Kevin

The 100-yard classroom : winning strategies for helping kids succeed in school, sports, and life / Kevin Kush. – 1st ed. – Boys Town, NE : Boys Town Press, 2007.

p. ; cm.

ISBN-13: 978-1-889322-87-2
ISBN-10: 1-889322-87-3

1. Sports – Psychological aspects. 2. Motivation (Psychology) 3. Coach-athlete relationships. 4. Teamwork (Sports) 5. Coaching (Athletics) I. Title. II. Hundred-yard classroom.

GV706.4 .K87 2007
796.01--dc22   0708

10 9 8 7 6 5 4 3 2 1

To every teacher whose classroom I have ever entered and to every coach I have had the pleasure to play for and learn from. From grade school to graduate school, all of you have had an enormous impact in shaping the man I am today. Thank you from the bottom of my heart.

TABLE OF CONTENTS

Acknowledgments

I would like to thank Mike Sterba for making this project a reality.

A big thanks to my Mom and Dad for helping build a better man, and to my two sisters for their continued support.

To my sons Keegan and Christian; everyday you give me a reality check as to what is truly important.

To my wife Lynne; thanks for the sacrifice it takes to be a coach's wife and for giving our family unconditional love. You are simply the best!

And finally, thank you to Girls and Boys Town for allowing me to share in its mission.

Note to Reader

Girls and Boys Town, the nation's largest privately funded program for severely at-risk, abused, abandoned, and neglected girls and boys was founded as Father Flanagan's Boys' Home in 1917 by Father Edward J. Flanagan. The nonprofit, nonsectarian home has youth care and health care programs that reach across the United States. From its humble beginnings in downtown Omaha, Nebraska, Father Flanagan and his boys built the community that became popularly known as "Boys Town," an incorporated Nebraska village. In 1975, Girls and Boys Town programs moved from dormitory-style living to family homes, and in 1979, its first girl residents were admitted. Expansion programs began in 1983 and now stretch to 19 sites in 15 states and the District of Columbia. In 2000, our children across the country voted to extend the name of our organization to "Girls and Boys Town" to recognize the scope of our programs.

Today, the Village of Boys Town is home to more than 500 children and is the national headquarters for programs that provide direct youth care and health care to more than 47,000 girls and boys annually. In addition to its long-term residential homes, Girls and Boys Town programs include short-term residential care, family-based and foster family services, and the Boys Town National Research Hospital, which specializes in services for children with hearing, balance, and communication disorders. The Girls and Boys Town National Hotline and the National Resource and Training Center assist more than a million children and families each year.

Boys Town, Nebraska, remains a destination for at-risk youth from across the country, and the Village schools continue to bear the town's name. The high school offers a full range of academic and athletic opportunities for both girls and boys, including the Cowboys football team coached by Kevin Kush.

Coach Kush,

I am writing you to thank you and say I appreciate everything. I have not had much of a male role model since my Pops was killed. Coach you help me set goals and work towards them. Being around you makes me want to do the right thing and work hard. I know I slip up here and there, but you have helped me alot. I really look up to you and you make me want to do the right thing. Coach you are one of the greatest men I have ever met. Not just coaching, but teaching and everything that comes with it. You may or may not here this alot, but I look at you as a father figure. I have never said it before and we may not know each other that well, but where I grew up there were not too many good people like you. I may not step foot on the field this whole season but I can say I have learned. Not just about football, but life. Everything you say to me is straight forward and it will help me in life. Thanks for all you do as a teacher and coach.

– FROM A FORMER BOYS TOWN FOOTBALL PLAYER

INTRODUCTION

THE TURNING POINT

"Make each day your masterpiece.
You have control over that."

– JOHN WOODEN
Coached UCLA to 10 NCAA basketball titles

I discovered my life's calling the way many people do: when I wasn't looking for it. I played football in high school and, after initially being recruited as a "walk-on," earned an athletic scholarship my second year in college. Following practice one day at the University of Nebraska at Omaha, the head coach asked if I would be willing to help out at a youth football clinic. I agreed. As soon as I started working with the kids at the clinic, I knew what I wanted to do. I wanted to be a football coach.

It wasn't long after the football clinic ended that I went to the university offices and asked what

I needed to do to change my major so that I could become a teacher. This was my path to coaching. I wasn't afraid or ashamed to admit (and I feel just as strongly about this today!) that I wanted to get involved in the education field so I could coach. Why? Because I knew in my heart and soul that coaching was the way I could help kids and have a positive influence on their lives. It was how I could make a difference.

After graduating from college, I accepted an offer to teach business education classes and a position as an assistant football coach at a large public high school in Omaha, Nebraska – a part of the country that lives and dies by its football teams. It was there that I met and learned from two great mentors – one in the classroom, Mike Logan, and the other on the football field, Gene Suhr.

Suhr, the head football coach, was one of the best, most successful, and most experienced high school coaches in the state. For nine years, I watched and questioned, listened and learned. He was always willing to stay late and answer my questions, and he challenged and encouraged me to become the best I could be in every aspect of coaching and helping young people. I worked hard and with passion. Over time, I earned my way from being a defensive assistant coach with a limited and focused amount of responsibility to a coordinator who was in complete control of the defensive side of the ball.

The team and the entire football program were second to none. We were a perennial power-house in the largest and most talented high school league in the state, competing with the best teams for championships. During my time there, we won many games, including a state championship; we were runner-up another year. We were good and always would be. The players and coaches were committed to competing at the highest level week in and week out, and we knew if we prepared well, we would win. All this was expected and demanded by those involved: players, coaches, administrators, and fans. Anything else was unacceptable.

In 1996, while I was teaching class, an unexpected phone call came to the high school office. It was a call that would change my life. Norm Ridder, the superintendent of schools at Boys Town, Nebraska, left a message asking me to call him back. When we talked, he said that some other coaches had recommended me as a young, energetic, and bright coach who would be a good fit for the head coaching position at Boys Town High School. He asked if I was interested in interviewing for the job. I was hesitant but agreed to come and visit the campus. I knew very little about the organization or what they did there other than it was a home for troubled children. Until that phone call, I hadn't even known they had a football team!

Almost immediately after arriving on campus, I knew this was a special place. It was obvious to the kids on campus that I was a visitor and at least three of them came up to say "Hello," introduce themselves, and shake my hand. This blew me away! I'd never felt so welcomed and appreciated by high school students.

During my visit, I learned that the Village of Boys Town is home to a residential treatment program now known as Girls and Boys Town that helps troubled and at-risk youth and their families. Kids who live there often are unmotivated and academically, behaviorally, and/or emotionally challenged. At Boys Town, boys and girls live separately in homes in a family-style environment where married couples provide the warmth, structure, and treatment necessary to allow healing to take place. The campus includes a high school and middle school, both with full academic and athletic programs. I learned that while some youth live at Boys Town for many years and graduate from high school there, the average length of stay for a boy or girl is about 18 months. This creates a unique challenge for coaches trying to build a successful football program year in and year out.

That night, I told my wife about the visit and all I had experienced and learned. We both knew immediately that Girls and Boys Town was where I was supposed to be – that a door had just opened for me and my family. But, I was stepping out of my comfort zone; how far out I would soon learn.

Success and winning at the highest level in high school football was second nature to me, so coming to Boys Town High School was a complete culture shock. The kids I was used to coaching were committed, self-motivated, hard-working, and already skilled from years of practicing and playing football. Boys Town's football team – called the Cowboys – played in a much smaller league. The talent level in the league and on the Cowboys' team dropped off dramatically from what I was accustomed to. Most players had never played organized football before.

We even had to teach players how to put on their pads and uniforms correctly! (It remains this way today.) Many days, I didn't know who would be at practice because if a youngster misbehaved badly enough at school or in his home, he wouldn't be playing football that day. I knew right away I had my work cut out for me, and that turning things around was going to take time and patience.

The Cowboys hadn't won a game the season prior to my arrival. My first year as head coach didn't produce a much better result: we won one game and lost eight. The team we did beat won only one game, too. We were easily one of the worst teams around – at any level – in all aspects of the game, both physically and mentally. All season long, I carried around a notebook and wrote down things that needed to change if the football program was to become successful. The list was long and included just about everything having to do with football.

Having a successful high school football team at Boys Town is important for many reasons. None is more important than the sense of pride it helps instill in the boys and girls who've led troubled lives. Most of these young people have not experienced success at home, in school, or on the field. All the kids – players and non-players – need something to cheer about so they can hold their heads high. Being part of something successful helps them grow and develop in ways I never dreamed. Creating a successful football program at Boys Town High School isn't so much about winning games as it is about creating feelings of worth and community.

When that first season was over, the administration asked me what needed to be done to fix things. I took out my notebook and rattled off the long list. It included everything from setting expectations for in-season and off-season behaviors to a greater emphasis on off-season weight training and game-day preparation. But, the most important change that needed to occur would be my biggest challenge: moving the players from **being involved to being committed**. The players were so used to losing that it didn't matter or hurt much anymore. It was easy for them to give up and lose when they ran into adversity on the football field because they weren't committed. They hadn't fully invested themselves physically, emotionally, mentally, or intellectually. The administration understood what I wanted to do. They shared my vision and gave me their full support.

That summer, we began the process of change – of moving the kids from being involved to being committed. The players were slow to trust and understand all of what I was demanding from them. After all, most of these youth had come from environments where adults who were interested in seeing youngsters succeed were few and far between.

I knew that the best way to gain the kids' trust in me and what I was doing was to simply keep plugging away every day. Modeling commitment for them was important. That meant spending extra hours and extra effort every day working with players and the team to improve. The standards I set to be a member of the Cowboy football team were high and demanding, and many players struggled with the changes. The foremost quality that could move a player from a "varsity candidate" to a "varsity member" was character. A player had to show the coaches that he could be trusted to do the right thing at home, at school, and on the field. Only the committed kids who displayed good character were allowed on the varsity field.

Later that summer, players started to comment that I was "always around." It was then I knew the tide was turning. The kids began to believe and trust that I really did care about them, and that I was committed to making them better as individuals and as a team. More and more players began to accept and respond to the higher standards. The spirit of commitment as players and as a team began to sink deeper into their minds and efforts. Most didn't even realize it was happening.

We lost our first game of the second season. But I saw signs of progress. Kids played hard to the final whistle, didn't give up or point fingers at each other when adversity hit, and continued to execute when the game was out of reach. These were all things they weren't capable of doing the previous year. Also, the loss stung the players; it hurt. This was another sign they were becoming more and more committed.

The next week we played the third-rated team in the state, a perennial powerhouse in our league. The game was on their home field – an intimidating atmosphere filled with rowdy fans. All the ingredients were in place for a drubbing.

The game turned out to be well-played, close, and exciting. In the final 30 seconds, we scored to retake the lead. After the ensuing kickoff, the opposing team had time for one last play. Their quarterback dropped back and heaved a "Hail Mary" pass that flew over my defensive backs' outstretched arms and hands. Their receiver caught the ball and quickly turned for the end zone. My heart was in my throat as I saw the game slipping away. Amazingly, at the last second, one of my players dove for the receiver's ankles and tripped him up – just four yards short of a miraculous game-winning score.

In my 20 years as a coach, it remains the greatest and most satisfying victory I've been associated with. Why? First, it simply wasn't supposed to happen. It was a total and complete shock – a true sporting upset. Second, the response from the players after the game was unlike anything I had ever experienced. Many lay sobbing on the field, overcome with emotion. They had worked so hard over the past year to improve and they had hit the jackpot! Finally, the game had a profound and undeniable impact on the positive direction of the football program. This one extraordinary game provided the fuel that propelled the players and team to strive each and every practice and game for the level of commitment needed to succeed.

We finished the season with eight wins and three losses and made the state playoffs. The following year, we went all the way to the state semi-finals. Over the past ten years, we've won at least eight games every year and have been a fixture in the Top

Ten ratings. In 2005, we won 11 games and again made it to the state semi-finals. And in 2006, we had another successful season and reached the second round of the state playoffs. Today, the players who join the football program learn from the players who went before them what it takes to be a Cowboy football player: character and commitment.

■ ■ ■

In the two decades I've been blessed to be a teacher and coach, I've discovered that coaching isn't just about wins and losses and the responsibilities that come with building a successful team. It's much more than that. It's about instilling character, values, and other important life skills to help kids become successful.

I've learned that the coaching hat isn't the only one a coach must wear. There are many other roles a coach has to fill in his players' lives. Coaches are teachers, mentors, counselors, encouragers, confronters, and comforters, just to name a few.

The playing field, I've found, is one of the most fertile grounds for teaching and learning to take place with young people. And I'm not talking just about athletic lessons. For most kids, most of the time, it's less about sports and more about how to go about living a responsible, productive life.

Along the way, I've learned many things about myself and how to get kids to work together as a team. As is typical in sports, there have been tremendous highs and gut-wrenching lows – both with the team and with individual youth. It hasn't been easy. That's okay; it comes with the territory. What's important is that I know I have made and am continuing to make a positive difference in many young peoples' lives. And that's a touchdown every time in my playbook!

The "It" Factor

"It" is a term we use in coaching to describe people who have a knack for success. This success isn't just about winning or losing games and championships here. I'm talking about coaches who are fully invested and committed to helping kids grow and succeed both on and off the field. Winning and earning accolades are simply (and usually!) byproducts.

The "It" factor isn't limited just to sports and coaching. Teachers, Scout leaders, parent volunteers, mentors, and other adults who work with children and teens in various learning settings can have "It." These folks possess a set of intangible qualities and a dedication to teaching and working with youth that inspires and motivates youngsters to learn and, ultimately, win in life. They genuinely care about kids and are willing to go the extra mile to help them grow and achieve.

It's easy to spot individuals who have the "It" factor. They have a visible burning passion for what they do; a desire to get the job done, no matter the obstacles they face; and the ability to grab kids' attention and hold them accountable. They know when to be tough with kids and when to pat them on the back, and they have the courage to be role models and do the right thing. This book discusses all these qualities (and more!), and offers ideas that can help cultivate and enhance the "It" factor inside of you in whatever area you are working in with children – education, athletics, music, Scouting, recreation, work, and more. These include suggestions on how to:

- Establish expectations.
- Set goals.
- Earn their trust.
- Overcome adversity.
- Establish boundaries.
- Invest time.
- Be prepared.
- Catch 'em being good.
- Practice the fundamentals.
- Seek improvement.
- Use role models.
- Build character.

Working with young people and helping them succeed is one of the most powerful, important, and satisfying vocations a person can be called to. You can never underestimate the influence and power you exercise in the lives of the youth who pass your way. I didn't really understand this until kids started sending me Father's Day cards and letters like the one at the beginning of this book. Youngsters need people like you in their lives, helping to guide them in the right direction and instilling in them skills, values, and character. So teach, care, and share your "It" factor with the kids in your life!

FIRST AND TEN

"The greatest accomplishment is not in never falling, but in rising again after you fall."

– VINCE LOMBARDI
Legendary coach of the Green Bay Packers

This book is about how adults can help young people move forward, reach goals, and succeed in any setting where learning takes place. There's an almost limitless number of times when kids have the opportunity to learn something new and grow, whether it's throwing a baseball correctly, understanding prime numbers, becoming skilled at building a fire as a Boy Scout, understanding lessons in a Bible study class, or playing a song on the guitar. Our responsibility is to teach kids how to move from point "A" to point "B." Point "A" is where each child starts his or her journey; point "B" is the destination.

Kids need help learning the process and steps necessary for successfully moving from point "A" to point "B." This process is not innate or instinctive to youth. It takes time, effort, and guidance from knowledgeable adults for youngsters to learn how to be successful in different areas of their lives, and to successfully navigate from start to finish.

Over the years, I've used a number of strategies to help kids move from a starting point to a successful and fulfilling end point. These strategies, laid out in the following chapters, work not only on the football field, but also can be (and have been) effectively applied in the classroom and other learning settings. They are practical and easy to use. In fact, adults in any child-learning setting can use these strategies to help kids move toward success: classroom teachers, music instructors, youth groups leaders, mentors, coaches at all levels, and others.

Fair Does Not Mean Equal

How many times have you heard this from kids? "That's not fair!" This declaration is an occupational hazard for those who work with and help children and teens. Often, kids may think a situation or decision is unfair because someone else is being treated differently than them. I tell kids that being treated fairly has nothing to do with being treated equally. Fairness means dealing with each youngster individually – and that usually leads to treating some kids differently. It also means that you take into account all the unique factors that make up a young person's life.

When it comes to learning, each and every kid has a unique starting point (or point "A") and ending point (or point "B"). Not every player can be the starting quarterback on the football team or an "A" student in algebra or the lead actor in the school play. When determining a person's starting and ending points, there are many individual factors to take into account. Some of these are:

- Age

- Developmental Level

- Intellectual Ability

- Emotional Level

- Physical Ability

- Natural or God-Given Talent

- Home Environment

- Family's Economic Status

- Motivation for Being Involved

All these factors can play key roles in helping kids set realistic and attainable starting and ending points. Many times, adult and kid worlds collide because these individual factors haven't been taken into consideration. For example, an adult may expect more from the child than he or she is capable of, or fail to provide enough of a challenge for the child. Either way, it can lead to misunderstandings and frustration for both kids and adults, and often results in kids wanting to give up or quit. The best approach is to treat kids as the unique individuals they are.

An example of this happened during my first year as the Cowboy head coach. I learned there were some boys who wanted to be part of the team simply so they could be recognized as a varsity football player. Their end goal was to wear a varsity football jersey to school on game days. They had no intentions of pushing themselves to become better players and contributing members of the team. So, the following year, we established specific expectations that required youngsters to work much harder (both during the season and in the off-season) to be considered a varsity candidate. And we made these expectations clear to all prospective players. Fewer kids came out for football the second year, but the ones who did were committed and had end goals far beyond just wearing a varsity jersey to school on game day.

It's also important to remember that there will be many starts and stops and small victories and losses. In order to successfully navigate and reach their destination, young people need to have short-term point "A's" and "B's" all along the way. Oftentimes, a child's point "B" is just one ending point – not **the** ending point. Striving toward and achieving goals is an ongoing, fluid process. Point "B" is usually an immediate short-term goal that might become the starting point for the next move forward. There are many small movements, steps, and short-term accomplishments that have to take place for a youngster to reach his or her ultimate destination or goal. For example, at the end of the first day of football practice, I don't expect to see a polished football team. That's the long-term goal. Instead, I'm more concerned with the small victories like teaching the players how to correctly put their pads in their uniforms or helping them understand and begin to master a drill. From there, we'll take another step forward and another and another until, ultimately, at the end of the season, the players have arrived as individuals and as a team at their long-term destination.

It's Okay to Explain Why

Coaches are notorious for telling the inquiring player, "Because I said so. That's why!" I've found that with today's kids it's much more effective to take a few extra minutes to explain the purpose of or reason behind what I'm asking them to do. Giving reasons has worked for me for years, both on the football field and in the classroom. When I take time to give reasons, students and athletes appreciate it, learn, and are much more likely to do what I ask of them.

There are times when young people just can't connect what they are asked to do with the reason for doing it, especially when the benefit to them is not immediate or readily apparent. They often fail to realize that good things will happen in the long run if they do what they're asked to do. Giving kids reasons helps to turn on that light bulb that allows them to see and understand the long-term connection.

Let me give you an example of how giving reasons has worked for me: There is usually one game every year when we play a team that our players know we should beat handily, even with a mediocre performance. There might be a tendency to let down that week in practice. So I give them a good reason to work hard. In practices the week leading up to this game, I push the players especially hard and challenge them to get better. Before practices begin that week, I'll hold a team meeting and explain that we're not only preparing for the next opponent but also for that tough and important game later in the year that really counts. A vast majority of the players respond positively and with a good effort when I give a reason like this, and in the end, that's all I'm looking for.

I also use reasons in the classroom. For example, I explain to my students why certain rules are in place and why I have certain expectations regarding classroom behavior. I frequently take the time to tell students why we're doing particular assignments and how they will help them with future content.

The point here is that whenever you have the opportunity, no matter the setting you're in, take time to explain and give reasons. This will help make your life much easier and your teaching more effective because you've provided kids with immediate "buy-ins." Trust me, reasons work! If they didn't, I would just tell the kids, "Do it because I said so!"

What Do You Bring to the Game?

No one's perfect. This is true in all aspects of life. And just as the young people you work with have their strengths and weakness, so do you. I believe our limitations are harmful only if we deny that they exist, because then we take no action to improve on them.

It's important for adults who work with kids to analyze and recognize what they're good at and what they need to get better at. For example, your strength may be that you have played and know a sport or musical instrument inside out. But you may be inexperienced when it comes to teaching and motivating kids. Or, you might be skilled at working with and motivating kids but have a little knowledge of what you're trying to teach. The best solution to both these situations that I know of comes from my experience in coaching. When I ask other coaches for help or advice in any area of the game, they gladly give me everything they've got. There's no holding back! Practices and office doors are wide open. Nothing is secret or sacred, whether it involves motivation, discipline, techniques, or strategy. I've also found this to be true in teaching.

The point here is don't hesitate to seek out mentors and ask them for advice and help. There's always someone with more experience or expertise than you out there, and he or she is almost always ready and willing to lend a helping hand. Let's face it: Kids know when you're faking it, so don't even try. Instead, remember that there are older and wiser mentors around who were once in your shoes. Most will be more than happy to open their doors and share their experiences with you.

"Just One Thing"

My assistant coaches and I attend football clinics throughout the year. We're always seeking ways to become better coaches, and clinics are great ways to share and gather information. When my assistants head off to a clinic, I ask them to bring back **just one thing** – a term or phrase, a motivational story to tell the players, an innovative drill or teaching technique, or even a whole new play. I tell them not to worry about bringing back everything because that's when they're likely to miss out on the one really important thing that will help us out the most.

As you read this book, I encourage you to do the same. Look for that one thing that can make the difference in your work with young people. All the strategies in the book can be helpful but they may not all apply to you or your situation. However, one or more chapters could have ideas, information, and/or suggestions that will help a lot.

No matter how many victories or successes you've had with kids, it's important to always strive to get better. The moment you relax and believe that you have it all figured out is the moment you begin to slide backward toward mediocrity. To continue winning with kids, keep moving forward by seeking and being open to new learning opportunities! I hope you make this book one of those opportunities.

There are 14 chapters in this book. Each chapter begins with an inspirational quote from a notable coach or athlete. Some of these people you might recognize and others you might not, so there's a short description about the person. They all have the "It" factor. I encourage you to read and learn more about these people. They're excellent role models who can provide additional information about how to teach and coach young people the right way.

CHAPTER 4

I'VE GOT YOUR BACK, YOU'VE GOT MINE

Strategy: Earn Their Trust

"The foundation of getting people to do what you want them to do, is built on a relationship based on trust."

> – MARTY SCHOTTENHEIMER
> *NFL head coach for more than two decades*

D uring my first football practice as the new head coach of the Cowboys, the players were filled with suspicion and unease. It was written all over their faces and showed in their actions. There were nervous looks and angry glares; many kids loafed through the drills and ignored my instruc-

53

tions and teaching. A few were even more unco-operative, disagreeing with certain things asked of them. They wanted to do everything their way. I understood how the players felt and why they acted like they did. As a matter of fact, I had anticipated this kind of reaction, so it really didn't bother me much. After all, the players didn't know me. I was just another new adult who suddenly appeared in their lives ready to bark out orders. I told my assistant coaches and the administration that there was no quick and easy fix here, and things would slowly get better. Understandably, the players didn't trust or believe in us and what we were asking them to do. The only way we could earn these things was by consistently working hard and showing them commitment over a long period of time. Players needed to see that the other coaches and I had the knowledge and expertise to make them and the team better. Equally important was demonstrating that we had passion for helping kids, cared about them, and had their best interests at heart.

From start to finish, the first season was a struggle, and we didn't get much accomplished in terms of wins. However, at this point, winning games on the football field was much less of a concern to me than winning the players' trust. It wasn't until the following summer, during conditioning, that I began to see the players let their guard down. I had been around for a year, and the players started to believe that my passion and drive to make them and the football program better was the "real deal." They saw me there every day continuing to teach them skills and encouraging them to improve. I wasn't going to give in or give up – and the players finally believed it. My assistant coaches and I continued to earn more and more trust and respect as time went on. We've built on this, and today have a trusting atmosphere filled with respect for and belief in what we are doing.

■ ■ ■

Many young people in today's society have had adults come in and out of their lives on a regular basis. A lot of these relationships end with kids feeling disappointed, let down, and hurt. As a result, they've learned to be suspicious and skeptical of new adults. It's a survival mechanism. Can you blame them?

A big key to helping youth succeed today lies in the "trust factor." This means that kids must come to believe in you and your abilities and what you're trying to teach them. Also, they need to believe that you care about them.

It's hard for kids today to trust. There are many reasons for this. They see TV programs and read stories about adults they should be able to trust who break the law and do awful things to kids. Also, the media – TV, music, videos, movies, magazines, computers, etc. – send negative messages to young people about trust and faith in others. But, by far, a youngster's immediate environment has the biggest impact on his or her ability to trust. Negative experiences with adults who are close have caused some kids to throw in the towel and make the blanket assumption that all adults are untrustworthy.

This is especially true for the students and athletes I teach and coach at Girls and Boys Town.

You will come across young people who've lost confidence in adults and have trouble trusting you. You may have to peel through layers of hurt and disappointment before kids begin to see you as genuine and the "real deal." In this chapter, we'll discuss how to get youth to buy into you as a trusting person and into what you're doing. The sooner you get kids to trust you and your ability to help them succeed, the sooner you'll both see positive results.

A Total Team Effort

Trust means that kids have confidence in you to lay out an effective blueprint for success and make the right decisions to help them meet goals. It also means they believe you care about them and won't hurt them, and that they can rely on you. When young people trust you, they can believe that you know what you're doing and that you will do what's best for them.

An important life lesson for kids is learning who they can trust and what they believe in. There are lots of "phonies" out in the world looking for vulnerable children to take advantage of and manipulate. Getting involved with these kinds of people can be unhealthy and even dangerous for youngsters.

Many young people simply don't know what's good for them or who's good for them. That's where you come in. Coaches, teachers, mentors, and other adults who work with and help kids have a tremendous opportunity – I would even say a responsibility – to teach them what a safe and trustworthy person looks like and acts like. The best way to do this is through teaching and modeling traits like trustworthiness, caring, respect, responsibility, fairness, and others when you interact with kids. As they gradually learn to identify these traits in others, young people begin to make better choices about the people they associate with and what they do with them.

Here are some other important benefits of teaching and building trust with kids:

- They buy into your teaching more quickly, which creates a better learning environment.

- It creates better relationships between you and your kids, resulting in fewer behavior problems.

- They find you credible and knowledgeable, and are more likely to do what you ask with less hassle and fewer complaints.

- Kids learn that it's not only okay to seek out or accept help from others, but that it's a necessary ingredient for moving from point "A" to point "B."

Trust the Plan

Young people are a lot smarter than we think, especially when it comes to recognizing genuineness. To put it bluntly, many kids are good at smelling out a rat. If they sense any bit of phoniness in you, you'll lose them and their trust very quickly. And once you've lost a kid or a group of kids, getting him or her or the group back on board is extremely difficult. That's why it's important to earn and build trust in an honest and patient manner. Stay committed to doing it the right way; shortcuts lead to disaster.

Here are some suggestions on how to build trust the right way:

- **KNOW YOUR JOB.** Kids come to adults for instruction and guidance in many specific areas: academics, music, dance, sports, Scouting, etc. Take time to learn every facet of what you do and how best to teach it so you can be as good a mentor as possible. We all have different gifts and interests. And sharing our knowledge of, experience with, and enthusiasm for our area of interest is rewarding and fun, especially when kids are eager to learn more. So learn and master your craft. Seek out your own mentors who have more knowledge and experience than you and ask them for words of wisdom, advice, and guidance. Trust me on this one. Mentors are out there, ready and willing to help; you just have to reach out to them. Also, increase your knowledge base and skills by reading books and magazines, researching Web sites and other information on the Internet, and attending advanced seminars or clinics. Doing all this can make you much more effective and successful with helping youngsters learn what you have to teach so they can reach their goals.

- **Do Your Job**. Know what you can and can't do, and what your responsibilities, limitations, and boundaries are. Then do your best to do what you've been trained to do. Don't fake it by trying to do more than you're capable of; this usually leads to problems and can be bad for kids. For example, when a student or player comes to me with a family or personal problem, I know that my responsibility is to listen and then to get him to someone who can provide the best help. For example, I had a player at Girls and Boys Town who started telling me about his relationship with his father and how terrible it was. I let the player talk a bit, told him I was sorry about the situation, and strongly encouraged him to speak with his Family-Teachers, who are trained to deal with these kinds of issues. I don't offer a lot of advice to kids on how to handle issues outside of football or the classroom because I'm not a trained counselor. Sure, I have my opinions, and sometimes it's hard to keep them to myself. But I know when to keep my nose out of something because I have no business getting involved and because it can just further muddle things up for kids. My point here is this: If you're a coach, help youngsters with sports. If you're a teacher, work to make your kids better students. If you teach music, help youth learn to play and master an instrument. Don't stray far from your area of expertise. And remember: When tough issues arise with young people (and they will!) that are outside your comfort zone and training, your main responsibility is to get kids to the person or people best qualified to help them.

- **BE PROFESSIONAL.** It's important to present yourself as an authority figure by how you dress, talk, and behave. Don't make the mistake of trying to be like the kids so they will like you. When you try to be their "friend" by dressing, talking, or acting like they do, you lose your authority and blur the boundaries between you and the kids. This kind of confusion isn't good for anybody. It's okay to be friendly with young people by treating them with kindness and respect, and by having fun and joking around with them. But, your focus should always remain on teaching and building positive, appropriate adult-child relationships.

- **BE CONSISTENT.** Your kids expect you to be the same person every day. That means you must address positive and negative situations in a calm, even-handed manner, and establish and reinforce a consistent approach to your teaching, coaching, mentoring, etc. It also means showing up on time and doing the best you can every day. This sounds like a cliché, but it's not always easy to do. There will be situations that arise in your personal and professional life that might threaten to spill over into your interactions with kids. You might become more easily frustrated or short-fused with them when they're least expecting it. When you allow this to happen on a regular basis, it's a surefire and quick way to distance yourself from your kids and give them a reason to distrust you. So, do your best every day to be steady and straightforward in how you interact with and treat them. When they know what to expect from you, young people are more likely to be comfortable, to let their guard down, and to trust you.

- **GO THE EXTRA MILE.** Take an interest in kids outside the setting you're in. I often take my two sons to watch kids who play football for me compete in other sports like wrestling and basketball. I show support by attending their games and cheering them on. When they see me doing this, it has a tremendous impact on them. It shows them that I care about them outside of football. I do the same thing for my players who act in a school play or sing in the choir. Also, you can talk to young people about other areas of their lives that are "safe," like how they are doing in school or how an extracurricular activity they participate in is going. Avoid personal issues like family matters or how a youth is getting along with his or her girlfriend or boyfriend. These are outside the appropriate boundary you want to set for you and your kids.

- **BE PATIENT**. This might be the hardest thing to do! I know it was for me when I first arrived to coach the Cowboys. I wanted my players to trust in me and what I was asking them to do right away so we could start building a winning football program. However, many times, things need to get worse before they get better. Rarely, if ever, is trust simply given to someone; it must be earned over time. So don't force things. Let it all unfold at its own pace. Be prepared to dig in for the long haul. It'll be worth the wait!

- **MAKE IT MUTUAL**. Trust is a two-way street. In order to work together in a spirit of trust and to achieve successful outcomes, you have to have as much faith in your kids as you want them to have in you. There will be setbacks; try to make sure they're only temporary. Set your expectations high, and work hard to convince young people that they can reach their goals. And remind them that they have to earn your trust, just like you have to earn theirs.

Huddle Up!

When you firmly establish trust between you and your kids, great things can happen. They will believe in you and what you're asking them to do, and they will work hard to meet your expectations and follow the plan you've helped put together for them to succeed. Trust also helps move girls and boys from being involved to being committed. Their level of performance improves and they stay the course when faced with adversity.

Remember that you only have control over what you do and say; you can't control kids and how they respond and act toward you. Do your part and be prepared to be both disappointed and amazed. Although some may choose a path filled with dishonesty, selfishness, and failure, many others will respond to you in a positive way and move forward toward their goals. Remain committed to teaching and modeling trust for kids and hope for the best out of them. Many times that's the best we can do.

"WARRIORS" AND "SLOBBERKNOCKERS"

Strategy: Overcome Adversity

"I've missed more than 9,000 shots in my career. I've lost almost 300 games. Six times, I've been trusted to take the game winning shot and missed. I've failed over and over and over again in my life. And that is why I succeed."

– MICHAEL JORDAN
Considered the greatest basketball player in NBA history; led the Chicago Bulls to six NBA Championships

---

One of my former football players, Robert, was born in Africa. His father was a political and military figure there. In a country plagued by poverty, the father feared for his young son's future and made the hard decision to give Robert an opportunity for a better life – and that meant Robert had to leave home and Africa. Robert spent a short time in Spain, then went to Texas where his uncle, a priest, helped get Robert accepted into Girls and Boys Town. When Robert came to live at Girls and Boys Town, he was a young grade school boy who had nothing – and he was all alone. His family couldn't provide support and encouragement during the times when he was troubled, struggling, lonely, and homesick. Also, Robert had received little to no schooling while in Africa and he didn't speak English. He certainly knew nothing about American football! The only football he knew involved a soccer ball. Here was a young boy ripped from his family, country, and culture and dropped into a totally foreign environment. I've never been associated with a youngster who had more obstacles to overcome than Robert.

Yet, he grew and thrived at Girls and Boys Town, and succeeded in many ways. On the football field, Robert arrived as a timid boy with zero experience in and knowledge of the game. But he was willing to listen and learn, and he soaked up everything we taught him at practice and during off-season workouts. Through hard work and determination, Robert molded himself into a football player. His senior year in high school, Robert left as one of the best football players I've ever coached. He earned a roster spot on and played in the annual Nebraska Shrine Bowl football game – an end-of-the-year all-star honor awarded to the best players in the state.

Robert graduated from Boys Town High School and went on to college where he earned degrees in business and foreign language. He continued to play football at the college level for several years before giving it up to focus on his studies. Today, Robert has a full-time job as a counselor at a local community college. He speaks four languages fluently. He also works part time for Girls and Boys Town, and he's the head coach of our junior varsity football team. This is his way of giving back to the place he loves. Recently, Robert saved enough money to go back to Africa to visit his family, something he hadn't been able to do since he arrived in America 13 years ago.

Robert was a prime candidate for failure. But with help and guidance, he chose the right path and shunned the lure of destructive forces like alcohol, drugs, and having children out of wedlock. Most people would have said that Robert had little to no chance of succeeding. But he persevered and beat the odds, despite what looked like crippling adversity. Robert's story is no different than that of Lance Armstrong or other famous people who've beaten the odds, and it's just as dramatic and inspiring to me and those who know him. I'm amazed by what he's accomplished and how he's gone about doing it. Robert always listened, learned, applied what he learned, and worked hard to overcome any perceived obstacles. He's a special kid who remains perpetually upbeat and enthusiastic. He's a positive force and a shining example of how to overcome adversity.

■ ■ ■

In our football program, we use some colorful terms to describe certain kinds of players and extraordinary events that happen on the field. For instance, a "slobberknocker" is a hit that's so hard and so nasty that the person on the giving or the receiving end is momentarily stunned – in other words, the player is knocked silly. A slobberknocker is an obstacle that can keep a player from staying in the game and accomplishing his goals. "Warriors" are players who deliver or take one of these vicious hits, but hop back up, shake out the cobwebs, and boldly play on, even though they know another big hit is just around the corner.

Robert was a warrior who overcame many slobberknockers, on and off the field.

As a coach, teacher, and parent, I have a fondness and appreciation for kids like Robert. They've learned the valuable lessons that slobberknockers can teach – that no obstacle is too big or too difficult to keep them from finding success.

Sometimes when a slobberknocker happens, young people don't want to get back up any time soon. In football, they might become gun shy and start avoiding contact, and this negatively affects their play. Or, in the classroom, they might let one bad grade get them thinking they're not smart enough to pass the class. The road to success is littered with obstacles – or slobberknockers – like frustration, setback, pain, and suffering. Let's face it, adversity is an unavoidable part of life. How kids perceive and handle it is the difference between success and failure.

Adversity can strike any facet of a young person's life – home, school, sports, extra-curricular activities, relationships, etc. When adversity does hit, kids can choose one of two paths: They can run and hide, or they can meet the challenge head on. Kids are much more likely to succeed when they face adversity straight on with courage and support, and the knowledge of how to go about doing it the right way.

Successfully overcoming obstacles is one of the most important life skills that parents, teachers, coaches, and mentors can teach young people. Without this skill, they are destined to a difficult and strained journey through life, one filled with frustration and failure. This chapter focuses on how you can teach kids to become warriors who overcome slobberknockers.

Grind It Out

Overcoming adversity is the ability to get back up when you get knocked down, whether it's physically, mentally, emotionally, or spiritually. Adversity is a natural and integral part of sports. There's an ebb and flow to games and seasons that mirrors the ups and downs of life. Adversity in sports can come in the many forms it takes on in life: injury, disappointment, loss, poor performance, and others.

The greatest gift of sports to its participants is the opportunity to learn how to overcome adversity in a safe and controlled environment where the outcome, good or bad, isn't crucial in the scheme of life. Sports can be a tremendous learning and training ground for teaching lessons about overcoming adversity that can be applied to other parts of kids' lives. Children can take these lessons into the future where the stakes are a bit higher and more meaningful, and where it can be tougher and more important to grind it out.

Many of my Cowboy football players are experts in overcoming adversity but don't even realize it. They have come from homes riddled with abuse, neglect, drug and alcohol abuse, and from neighborhoods rife with danger and crime. In their young lives, they've already experienced and overcome many more hurdles than most youth their age.

During a particularly rough point in the season or during halftime of a game, I make it a point to talk about adversity with my players. I tell them they are already successful in beating the odds because they have survived, are alive, and are working to make their lives better. Because they've gotten this far, the obstacles that football presents are a piece of cake.

When I do this, almost all the players nod their heads in understanding and respond by putting forth a greater effort with a more optimistic outlook. My point here is that it's important for you to tell and show kids how and when they've conquered obstacles. Many times, they don't even realize what they've done and don't always know they have the strength to be resilient and fight though tough times, regardless of past or current circumstances.

Make Lemonade Out of Lemons

Another part of teaching kids how to overcome adversity involves how you react and what you do when you run up against roadblocks and disappointments. This is a test of a person's true character. Overcoming adversity demonstrates a person's toughness, strength, courage, and resiliency, important traits for you to model and for young people to learn and develop if they are to grow and succeed.

I'll bet you've heard this before: You learn more from your failures than you do from your victories. Why is this? Well, with success comes a feeling of satisfaction. When satisfied, people tend to stop looking for ways to improve. Over time, they begin to take shortcuts and go through the motions. It's only human to stop working hard when everything's going your way. Eventually, however, this approach to life catches up to you and people stumble and fall.

When you experience setbacks and failure, it forces you to examine what you're doing and how you're going about doing it. To get back on top and experience success again, you now have to adjust and change. This happened to me and our football team in 2006. Going into the final game of the regular season, we were rated number one in the state in our class. We had a great group of individual athletes at the start of the year and our expectations were high. Over the course of the season, several key players made poor decisions and choices in school and at home that resulted in their dismissal from the team. I lost more players in 2006 than in any other season of my coaching career.

By the end of the year, we were holding the team together with bailing wire and duct tape. We lost our last regular season game and won one game in the state playoffs before being eliminated. It was a frustrating and disappointing end to a once-promising season.

While we were disheartened that the team didn't meet our expectations, my coaches and I used the situation as an opportunity to improve. After reviewing the year, I realized that what was missing from the team was a sense of "caring" between the players. They never really bonded together the way great teams do. And some didn't care that the bad choices they made would negatively effect other players and the team. As a result of all this, my coaches and I adjusted and changed how we go about building team unity. We have developed activities and exercises – both on the field and in the classroom – that teach and instill the character trait of "caring" among teammates. We used a setback as a springboard to doing our jobs better.

I tell my players and students that setbacks can turn out to be the best things that happen to them because failure will make them re-evaluate and change. It forces them to take lemons and make lemonade out of them. If they want success, they have to accept what happened, look for ways to improve, and take the necessary action to change.

Lots of people, kids especially, don't like change. But they become more willing to listen and make necessary changes when life's given them lemons. It's hard for adults who are close to and care for young people to watch them experience the pain and suffering that comes with failure. But it's okay – and most times necessary – to allow kids to experience failure. As adults, we have to convince youngsters that these experiences are learning opportunities. For a lot of kids, failure or the threat of failure are the only things that motivate them to try something new. And when they become open to change and your teaching, you can swoop in to help them put the pieces back together.

Treat Kids as Individuals

Adversity comes in many shapes and sizes, and it hits and affects every kid differently. For example, misplacing a homework assignment or getting a poor grade on a quiz can send some kids into a tailspin, while other kids take the events in stride. Because individuals respond to adverse situations in unique ways, it's important for you to get to know each one of your kids.

Never discount a situation or circumstance as being unimportant to a child because it doesn't seem important to you. What you consider insignificant may be a disaster to some kids. It's especially important to be aware of the young people who struggle with what appear to be minor issues or setbacks. These kids will require more of your time and teaching because it's more of a challenge for them to work through obstacles and move on. So, avoid the mindset that all kids see and react to adversity in the same way, and provide help when necessary, one child at a time.

March Down the Field

There is no magical formula for overcoming adversity. Nor are there specific steps to follow, like in goal-setting. The ways people deal with and overcome obstacles are wide and varied. What might work well for one person could spell disaster for another; it all depends on the person and the specifics of his or her situation.

There are, however, some common suggestions or guidelines for successfully handling adversity that can be extremely beneficial to the young people you work with. I've found these to be helpful when I talk with my players and students about how to overcome slobberknockers. In the remainder of the chapter, we'll discuss these approaches and how to use them. Planting these ideas in kids' minds and teaching them how to put them into action is a big step toward moving them toward **warrior** status.

Prepare Kids for Sudden Change

It's usually not a matter of "if" adversity will strike but "when." "Sudden change" is the phrase I use with my players and students to explain adversity. In a football game, our opponent might break a long run for a touchdown or our offense might fumble the football on our own five-yard line. In the classroom, a student who studied hard and prepared well for an algebra test might learn the next day she received a failing grade because of a silly mistake. Or, in the social world, a girlfriend or boyfriend might unexpectedly break up with a youth. To successfully deal with these kinds of adverse situations, young people first have to be prepared for sudden change.

When things are going great, it's easy to be upbeat and positive. During the season, there are times when my players and team bask too long in the wake of a win or a string of wins. Everything is rolling along smoothly and the players are content and satisfied. During these times, I challenge my players to think about and prepare for the inevitable times in the future when things aren't going to go their way. I ask them to envision how they will react and what they'll do when they're behind by two touchdowns with time running out, or when they've just lost a heartbreakingly close game or were beaten soundly because they played poorly.

The purpose of preparing for sudden change is to teach kids that adversity is unavoidable, that it *will* strike, and that they need to be ready when it happens. Being prepared is essential because it:

- Lessens the impact and shock, which allows for quicker recovery time.

- Helps youth stay focused and motivated to work hard so that lack of preparation isn't a reason for setbacks or failure.

Give Pre-Game Talks

Once young people understand the inevitability of sudden change, you can teach them the best way to react and what to do in certain situations before they occur. This "pre-teaching" helps kids understand that there are some aspects of a sudden change situation they can control, even if there are many others they can't.

One of the most important things kids can control during adversity is their own behavior – how they react and what they say and do. Before football games, we stress to our players that they have no control over the officials, and that they will make calls that will go for us and against us. We discuss how we expect our players to behave when an official's call leads to sudden change – our players are to keep quiet and, if spoken to, nod their heads or respond with a respectful voice tone. As a matter of fact, we tell the players to pretend like the officials aren't even there. This helps them to understand that they can't control others or issues that are outside their own actions and reactions.

Two other things kids can control are preparation and effort. Some students and players become very results-oriented and get discouraged easily when they don't hit the mark. For example, the best grade some of my students might ever get is a "B." They might not be among those students who are gifted with a superior memory or a natural ability to compute numbers. So, when students get upset because they're not getting all "A's," we talk about their preparation and effort. If they are preparing as well as possible and are giving their best effort on a test or assignment, then that's all they can control – and it's all I expect from them. If good quality preparation and effort are there, the results will take care of themselves.

Prepare Kids for Speed Bumps

I tell students and athletes to view disappointments and setbacks simply as "speed bumps" on the road to success. Everyone hits them at one point or another. Speed bumps might jostle you around a bit and slow you down, but they don't have to stop you from moving forward. There's a saying that sums up this concept very well: "A bend in the road is not the end of the road unless you fail to make the turn." Teach kids that they will have to make choices and adjustments along the way; it's all part of the journey.

It's important for young people to learn that no matter how bad things seem, over time, they *will* get better. When I explain this to my students and players, I use the analogy of having the stomach flu. When it first comes on, you feel pretty lousy and you might temporarily even feel worse. But in the end, you get better and recover. It's the same thing when adversity hits. When it first strikes, kids are likely to be anxious and discouraged. They might even want to give up. When this happens (and it will!), encourage kids to hang in there, and show your support by helping them work toward a positive outcome.

Keep in mind that problems aren't likely to be resolved as quickly as kids would like. Most youngsters have the mindset, "I want what I want and I want it now." Unfortunately, life just doesn't work that way. Successfully working through adverse situations takes time; most problems aren't solved overnight. That's why it's important to teach kids that patience is the key. Patience isn't a quality or skill that many young people possess, so be prepared to help them slow down, not rush or force things, and learn to let things unfold as they should.

Tell Stories

Kids of all ages (and adults too) enjoy hearing how others have beaten the odds. Stories of triumph over adversity inspire and motivate, and give kids the hope and strength to keep moving forward. There are lots of these stories out there – both of famous and not-so-famous people. Your job is to find them. The good news is that it's really easy to do. You can find stories in newspapers, magazines, books, TV shows and documentaries, movies, and on Web sites. Gather the stories and share them with your kids. Most of the stories I gather and share with my students and players show how others have overcome tremendous obstacles, obstacles that were much worse than anything my students and players have faced. This helps them to believe that they can succeed, too. (This concept is discussed in more detail in Chapter 12, "Heroes Not Zeroes.")

Be a Role Model

This idea is simple but very powerful: Show young people through your own reactions and actions how to go about overcoming obstacles. In other words, be a warrior yourself! When you work with kids, you will experience slobberknockers like frustration, disappointment, and failure, just like the kids. Think of these times as tremendous role-modeling opportunities when you can teach youth valuable lessons about adversity and how to handle it the right way. For example, as a football coach, I have to model how to overcome obstacles during every game. When sudden change occurs in a game, I have to pay attention to things like my facial expressions, voice tone, word choice, gestures, and so on. I have to be aware of my behavior and model how to remain calm and positive. I also have to model how to use good problem-solving skills when I'm frustrated and under pressure. What I do during these adverse times is sometimes a better lesson for my players than anything I could say to them. Kids need to see people – especially the authority figures in their lives – *live* what they talk about. Only then does it become the "real deal" to them.

Be in Their Corner

In boxing, there's a person called a "corner man." This person trains the boxer, provides strategy before and during the fight, helps treat injuries, and gives encouragement all along the way. All young people need a good "corner man," especially when they face adversity. There are plenty of "naysayers" and "doom-and-gloomers" out there. Don't be one of them! These people really have no business working with and helping kids. They limit potential and drag kids down. Instead, youngsters need people in their lives who are upbeat, enthusiastic, and willing to help them get up when they get knocked down.

Help Them Practice Getting Back Up

I like to set up situations that stress success right after failure has occurred. This is one of the most fertile times for learning to take place. Why? Because failure opens up most kids to change and makes them more willing to put forth greater effort. For example, when my team performs poorly and struggles with passing the ball during a game, I'll start off the next practice with something the team does well, like running the ball. This gives the players and team a shot of confidence before we begin working on our weaknesses. If the first thing you focus on or magnify is the problem area, kids become defensive and leave discouraged – this negatively affects effort and execution. So, take the sting out of correcting problem areas by highlighting and praising the positives first. You'll find that young people will be much more receptive to your teaching.

Let 'Em Pout and Move On

This is a great strategy to use with kids in any learning setting. Heck, I even use it with my assistant coaches! When people experience disappointment and failure, it's almost impossible for them to bounce back immediately and start again with great determination and effort. Kids and adults need time to grieve and process what happened before they're ready and able to get back at it. However, they can't wallow in self-pity forever. So, introduce and use a "pout period" with your kids. Give them a specific amount of time when they are allowed to pout and whine about a setback. Once time is up, their focus must shift solely to the present and what needs to be done to improve. Following a loss in football, I give my players 12 hours to mope around and complain about what happened during the game. After that, I expect them to put the loss behind them and to show up for practice the next day ready to work hard on moving forward.

Help Kids Develop Rhino Skin

Some young people can be so sensitive or easily discouraged that they allow even the most minor setbacks to stop them in their tracks. Sometimes, they never really get any positive momentum going again. You can encourage these kids to develop a thicker skin – or what I like to call "rhino skin."

In the animal kingdom, the rhinoceros is a massive creature known for its exceptionally tough hide. When you're motivating kids to tackle obstacles, tell them to imagine they have "rhino skin." Tell them this skin is so thick and tough that most of life's little irritations and troubles just bounce right off them. I do this with my players all the time. The message you send to kids is that they don't have to let every minor obstacle affect them so deeply that they want to give up and quit. Now, this doesn't mean you become insensitive or downplay or ignore their needs and feelings. You still should show empathy and help out when they're feeling down and out. But by consistently using the phrase "rhino skin" as part of a motivational strategy, you can encourage young people and remind them that they can get beyond the little things that keep them from moving forward.

My son, Keegan, is a great kid who strives to do well in school, sports, and all the activities he undertakes. Sometimes, his desire to succeed and achieve is dampened because someone gives him corrective feedback. When these situations arise, we talk about staying positive and not taking feedback personally, and how his teachers and coaches care and want to help him improve and reach his goals. I've even given him a small plastic rhino to put on his desk at home to remind him to keep feedback in proper perspective, shake it off quickly, and move on. It's really helped him to develop that tougher layer.

Talk Success

When you talk with kids about an adverse situation, use positive words and phrases that stress success. For example, when I address my team before a football game, I use the phrase, "When we win..." to start off many of my sentences. In school, you can say things like, "When you graduate..." or "After you nail this test...." It's so easy to do, and there are many ways you can use this kind of "positive speak" with students and athletes. This upbeat, positive way of talking rubs off on kids and gives them extra confidence, while also sending the message that you believe in them and their abilities, and that you expect them to succeed.

Huddle Up!

Knowing how to overcome adversity – being a warrior – is one of the most important life skills young people can learn. Without it, they can become lost and spiral into a cycle of disappointment, setback, and failure. Learning how to conquer life's slobberknockers enables kids to accomplish great things, even when they face daunting challenges. So, take the strategies and ideas presented in this chapter, apply them in your learning setting, and watch your kids turn into warriors like Robert!

TAKE CHARGE
Strategy: Establish Boundaries

"That's what I do now: I lead and I teach.
If we win basketball games from doing that,
then that's great, but I lead and teach.
Those are the two things I concentrate on."

– MIKE KRZYZEWSKI
Duke University head basketball coach since 1981;
led his teams to ten Final Fours and won three NCAA Championships

---

When I first entered the classroom as a teacher, I was 23 years old. I was young and filled with enthusiasm and hope for educating young minds. Like most new teachers, I desired to be both liked and respected by my students. I even remember wanting to be perceived as one of the "cool" teachers. I thought that by being more like a friend to my students, they would behave well and respond positively to my teaching. Man, was I ever wrong! Rather than responding with positive behavior, the students took advantage of my inexperience with discipline and structure in the classroom. The atmosphere was too loose and the students jacked around too much, pushing bad behavior to the limits. I became very frustrated because my classroom wasn't filled with respectful child-to-adult interactions and high-quality teaching and learning. I was dealing with a lot of unacceptable behavior, and this was cutting into the amount of time I had to teach academics.

I knew things needed to change. So I sought the advice of a mentor who had years of teaching experience. He helped me understand that in order to create a better learning environment, I had to toss out the notions that I needed to be a friend to students and be perceived as cool. Instead, I had to begin managing my classroom like a professional teacher. This meant I had to be an authority figure – someone who developed and set behavioral and performance standards, and delivered consequences (both positive and negative) when those standards were met or not met.

Immediately, I changed the way I went about running my classroom. First, I changed my approach to how I wanted students to perceive me. I was their teacher – an authority figure – not their buddy. Next, with the help of my mentor, I wrote up classroom expectations, rules, and consequences. I introduced all these to the students, and we discussed how the classroom environment would change. Finally, I committed to being a teacher whose main focus was on creating an environment where kids could learn and succeed. Being liked and seen as cool were no longer objectives for me. It took a bit of time for the students to adjust – less time than I had anticipated – and things got better. Student behavior improved and my job satisfaction increased dramatically. My classroom ran smoother and I had more time to teach. As a result of all this, student performance improved. Even the students were happier!

Over the years, I've continued to run and manage my classroom and football team the same way, with positive results. Today, I'm not concerned whether my students and players like me all the time – and they don't, especially after they receive a negative consequence. However, they do respect me as the authority figure who runs the classroom and team in a way that will help them learn and achieve. In the end, everyone wins when adults and young people know who's in charge!

■ ■ ■

During that first year of teaching, I learned some hard lessons about the importance of establishing appropriate boundaries with kids. Most adults who are new to working with young people frequently struggle with this issue. In many coaching and learning settings, adults are unsure about how they should act and interact with kids. They face a common dilemma: They want kids to like them, but they also want the respect that an authority figure must command.

This dilemma can lead to some interesting extremes. Some adults err by acting like the "tough guy." They interact in an extremely rigid and strict manner, which distances them from the kids, who see them as punishing and negative. More adults, however, try to be the "good guy." They treat kids like buddies, are too lenient, and get too involved in their personal lives.

Wanting to be the "good guy" is understandable. It's human nature to want to be liked, especially when you start working with a new group of children. Rarely, however, will this approach result in or lead to the respect that adults want and need from youngsters in order to create efficient and successful learning environments. Having good relationships with young people doesn't automatically result in earning respect from them. Focusing too much on creating and maintaining friendly relationships can lead to kids trying to manipulate adults, and the adults ending up frustrated and disappointed. In order to create and maintain a first-rate learning setting, you need to establish a healthy professional distance or boundary between you and the kids. Over time, as they come to see and believe that you care about them, and that your main focus is on helping them learn and succeed, they'll come to appreciate and respect you.

Stay Inbounds

On the football field, in the classroom, and in other learning environments, it's important for you to establish who's in charge right off the bat. As the authority figure, you're responsible for establishing and maintaining behavioral and performance standards in your setting. Kids need to know that you're the one who'll lead them on their learning journey, and that you'll hold them accountable for meeting expectations. Ultimately, this is what young people need to help them learn, meet goals, and succeed.

There are other important benefits that come from setting and maintaining appropriate boundaries with kids. Let's go over a few of them:

- Boundaries help bring order to learning settings. Someone has to be in charge and make the tough decisions and choices. And that person is you, not the kids! When boundaries are established and maintained, it's clear to youngsters what you expect from them and what they can expect from you.

- Appropriate boundaries between you and your youth model for them healthy adult-child relationships. This helps young people learn to distinguish between good relationships and ones that might be harmful.

- Appropriate adult-child boundaries and interactions enable kids to understand that you care about them, and that you believe in their ability to achieve goals and succeed. This helps them feel safe, secure, and worthwhile.

- When youngsters know the boundaries and what consequences to expect, effective teaching and learning can take place. There are fewer challenges to your authority because they know the limits.

You Don't Have To Buddy Up

In the process of establishing appropriate boundaries, a relationship will develop between you and your kids. But don't be disappointed if the relationship is not a friendship. Friendships are based on equality and a fair balance of power and control between people. That kind of relationship cannot exist between adults and kids in a learning setting. As an authority figure, you're in charge of setting expectations, deciding on rules, and delivering consequences. This means you have all of the control and power. There should not be an equality or balance to the relationship between you and your students. This is exactly what successful teachers, coaches, and other mentors create and maintain in effective learning environments.

To put it bluntly, young people don't need to like you as a friend (or at all for that matter) for successful learning to take place. It's nice if they do, but it's not a necessity. And it's unrealistic to think or expect that every child you work with will like you all the time.

When I ask adults about the person who had the biggest impact and positive influence on them while growing up, they always describe an adult authority figure like a teacher, coach, or other mentor – and not a peer or friend. These people tell me that their mentors cared enough to be willing to be the "bad guy" when they had to. In other words, these authority figures held their youth accountable, even if it meant they had to give negative consequences that occasionally made the youth upset or mad. These mentors also were willing to push and encourage them to meet their goals and reach beyond their potential. Usually, the adults I'm talking to remember being upset with their mentors many times. But over the years, they've grown to appreciate what these folks did and the sacrifices they made.

Let's face it, kids are fickle. One minute, they think you're the greatest, and the next, they treat you like their enemy. This usually happens because they didn't get what they wanted or because they earned a negative consequence. Don't take this behavior personally. It's just what young people do when things don't go their way. When they get upset with you (and they will!), remember to act in a professional manner – remain calm, respectful, and fair.

Kids have plenty of opportunities to make friends with other kids. They really don't need adults, especially ones who are authority figures in their lives, to be their friends. This doesn't mean that you can't enjoy kids' company by spending some time laughing and joking with them. They love this kind of behavior because it allows them to see you as being approachable. But, you still must be careful to maintain proper boundaries in all kinds of situations and interactions. That means keeping your humor and joking around inbounds and appropriate.

Wear the Black Hat

Don't be afraid to wear the "black hat." This means staying strong and committed if you have to deliver negative consequences. Giving negative consequences when youth deserve them won't irreparably harm your relationship. What will cause problems is not being consistent when correcting behavior, playing favorites, or letting misbehaviors go.

I learned this the hard way with one of my classes. The class was made up of football players and other students, all of whom were friendly, good-natured, and respectful. It was one of those good groups that teachers enjoy working with.

I expected all my students to be on time for class. If they arrived late, they earned a tardy. In this particular class, I started to let the rule and consequence slide. Instead, I'd joke with kids who were late and tell them to hurry up next time. Over time, more and more youngsters started arriving late with all sorts of excuses, and I began to get frustrated. When about half the class was late one day, I knew what I had to do. I told the kids that the rule and the consequence were back in effect – no exceptions. The problem was quickly resolved.

Consistency is the key. When you see young people mess up, don't hesitate to deliver a full and fair consequence. Kids know when they've made a mistake and, if you've been consistent, they understand that a consequence is most likely headed their way. However, if they've learned that you can be persuaded to go easier on them or drop the consequence altogether, they'll give it their best shot to get out of it. (Kids will do just about anything to get out of a negative consequence – cry, tell sob stories, make excuses, blame others, yell, accuse you of being unfair, and many other tricks of the kid trade.)

Your job is to avoid getting baited into discussing issues that have nothing to do with the situation at hand, which is a youngster's inappropriate behavior and the consequence he or she has earned. If you want to lose your students' respect real fast, just let them manipulate you to drop a consequence they've earned. Trust me, kids love to brag to their buddies about how they got one over on a teacher or coach. And, they'll share their secrets and strategies with other kids on how to get to you. So, stay alert and focus only on the inappropriate behavior and the consequences. All the other stuff is usually just a smoke screen.

Having said that, there will be times when kids feel they have a legitimate beef with you. The best thing to do is to tell them to come back at a later time when emotions have calmed down so you can talk with them about the issue. If they really feel something is unjust or unfair, they'll come back. But guess what happens most of the time? Nothing. That's right! Once they've calmed down, they realize they don't have a case and accept your decision. Don't be afraid to wear the black hat! Stay true to yourself and the kids by consistently correcting behavior and delivering consequences when they misbehave.

A Winning Formula

Boundaries are different for different settings. For example, what I say, how I say it, and how I act on the football field is far different from what I say and do in the classroom. On the field, when I'm teaching and coaching, I tend to talk to players more directly and in a louder, more authoritative voice. This is a boundary that works well in sports, but doesn't translate too well to the classroom. There, I use less confrontational words and a softer voice tone when I'm teaching, correcting student misbehavior, or giving students feedback on their performance. The real key to establishing effective boundaries is knowing your learning setting and determining what will work best to get your kids to respond to you and your teaching in a positive manner.

Let's go over some ideas and suggestions that you can use to develop, establish, and maintain boundaries that are appropriate, healthy, and constructive for you and the youngsters in your setting.

■ **FROM THE VERY FIRST DAY, LET KIDS KNOW YOU ARE STEERING THE SHIP.** It's much easier to establish your boundaries right away than to go back and try to fix them later. Let kids know your expectations for behavior, performance, rules, and consequences (both positive and negative) before you begin teaching any content. When everyone knows who's in charge and what to expect, you've set up a learning environment where youth can be successful.

- **USE A POSITIVE INTERACTION STYLE WITH KIDS.**
Avoid the negative "It's-my-way-or-the-highway"
approach to teaching and coaching. This dictato-
rial style turns young people off, alienates them
from you, and leads them to tune out anything
you have to offer. Instead, be upbeat, positive,
and optimistic in your interactions.

- **GIVE REASONS.** It's natural for kids to ask "Why?"
And it's okay for you to explain to them your reasons for doing certain things and having certain
expectations. Be prepared to answer legitimate
questions in a way that clearly describes to kids
how they will benefit from following rules and
meeting expectations as they pursue their goals.

- **LET KIDS KNOW THAT YOUR JOB IS IMPORTANT
TO YOU AND THAT YOU ARE SINCERE ABOUT
HELPING THEM LEARN AND SUCCEED.** I tell my
players I was hired to teach and coach them in
the game of football, and that I take my responsibilities very seriously. I also tell them that many
of the skills they're learning in football will help
them succeed both on and off the field. I want
my players and our team to win football games
because it allows them to experience the success
that can come from setting goals and working
hard to meet them. When kids see my passion
for coaching and teaching, they come to believe
that I'm the authority figure who knows what it
takes to help them succeed, and that I really care.

- **DO WHAT YOU WERE HIRED TO DO OR VOLUN-
TEERED TO DO.** One important aspect of your job
as a teacher, coach, or mentor is to have good
control of your learning environment. The key is
to avoid uncertainty and chaos, which can ruin
any learning setting. Everything that happens in
your learning environment is your responsibility.
So take the reins and take charge! Young people
expect you to do this, and if you don't, look out,
because they will!

- **EXPECT KIDS TO POKE AND PROD TO SEE IF YOU
ARE FOR REAL AND REALLY IN CHARGE.** One of
our expectations during every football practice
is that players must jog from one station or drill
to the next. Walking is not allowed. Jogging
builds good "hustle habits" for games, allows us
to get in more repetitions during practice, and
helps with conditioning. Every year, kids test this
expectation when they get tired. My coaches and
I stay on top of it by giving words of encouragement for those who do hustle and consequences
for those who don't.

Kids think they have a duty to check out the
boundaries every now and then. And, it's your
job to let them know that they're still in place.
Do this professionally and keep your head about
you. Don't let kids' misbehavior get under your
skin. Taking things personally can lead to unpro-
fessional conduct that can be damaging and
destructive to your relationships with young-

sters. Instead, expect misbehavior to occur and use teaching and negative consequences to correct it when it happens.

- **REMEMBER THAT YOU AND YOUR STUDENTS ARE NOT EQUALS.** Don't act like you are, and don't treat a child like your equal. Instead, remain respectful and fair, but always be confident, clear, and in charge.

- **AVOID ACTING, TALKING, AND/OR DRESSING LIKE THE KIDS.** You are not their peer. You are a professional, so act, talk, and dress like one!

- **DON'T BE AN EXPERT IN EVERYTHING.** Stick to what you know. It's okay to listen to personal issues and/or problems kids might be experiencing; but don't get over-involved and try to offer solutions outside your area of expertise. Instead, guide them to the person or people who can best help them. If you do offer words of wisdom, stick to universally sound advice like "Put your best foot forward"; "Think before you act"; "Talk to your parents or a relative who you trust about this issue"; etc. These are safe words of advice that can help young people move toward positive and productive solutions.

Huddle Up!

Popularity isn't a necessary ingredient in the recipe for effective teaching and coaching. For many adults who are new to working with kids, this is a tough truth to grasp. Many times, it's only through growing pains that adults come to understand this. What is crucial to building and maintaining a good learning environment is establishing clear boundaries, ones that let youngsters know you're in charge and that you have specific expectations and rules they need to meet.

Let's be realistic here. As adults, we all have bosses and authority figures whom we have to answer to, and they have boundaries and expectations they want us to meet. Teachers, coaches, and mentors can help kids learn valuable life skills by creating the same environment. This means setting and maintaining appropriate boundaries and expectations for kids that fit your learning setting.

Don't worry about whether or not young people like you. If you have their respect, and they know you're behind the wheel, you can help take them wherever they want to go.

TIME INVESTMENT EQUALS TOTAL COMMITMENT

Strategy: Invest Time

"There are 86,400 seconds in a day. It's up to you to decide what to do with them."

– JIM VALVANO
Former North Carolina State basketball coach who led his team to an upset win in the 1983 NCAA Championship game; died of cancer at age 47; founder of the "V Foundation," which is dedicated to finding a cure for cancer

---

My first Cowboy football team spent very little time working to improve. Their weightlifting, conditioning, and skill-improvement drills were poor during the off-season, and their effort didn't improve much at practices and games. The time and commitment the players put in to get better individually and as a team were minimal at best. And the results showed on the field – eight losses and one win. Following one loss, I walked into the locker room and saw players laughing, joking, and jacking around like it was the last day of school. There was absolutely no disappointment or frustration in the room – two things I commonly saw on the faces and in the body language of players on my former teams who were committed to excellence and success. To those players, losing stung and lingered. With my Cowboy players, however, getting beat and failing didn't seem to faze them one bit. It didn't take me long to figure out why they were so unaffected by playing poorly and getting beat. The players' and team's expectations reflected their failure to invest the time, energy, and effort necessary to develop any kind of commitment to achieve. Football was just another activity in their day, something to do and get out of the way. So, when they lost, they didn't care – and it certainly didn't hurt.

In order to build a successful program, this culture of apathy had to change. So, after the final whistle of the last game, I instituted new responsibilities and obligations that the players were required to meet. These activities increased the amount of time players spent on football-related drills and conditioning, both during the season and in the off-season. I hoped that spending more time improving and working toward success would lead to a deeper level of commitment. All this would, in turn, help create an atmosphere of excellence and a program where goal attainment was not just encouraged but expected. The off-season was now filled with mandatory drills, workouts, and classroom learning about how to compete with character.

During the first two weeks of the preseason, we held demanding two-a-day practices where only those with strong commitments would thrive and survive. During the season, the players were required to spend more time on the practice field, and they had to condition and train with greater effort and intensity. Kids began to see that if they wanted to play football for the Cowboys, they had to be willing to put in the time, give the extra effort, and stay committed. The players who were unwilling to meet these expectations left the team. It was their choice and there were no hard feelings. The roster began to fill up with players who were driven to give it their all, both physically and mentally, and who were fully invested in improving, achieving, and winning. As a result, the players and team improved dramatically the second year. We had an incredibly successful season – an 8-3 record and two wins in the state playoffs – that heralded a remarkable turnaround in our football program. Today, time, effort, and commitment permeate our program and are hallmarks of our teams.

■ ■ ■

Both adults and young people have certain responsibilities they have to take care of in life, like earning money at a job or working to get good grades in school. They also have other outside interests they enjoy doing and participating in, like singing in a choir or playing a musical instrument, being involved in a sport or club, cooking or gardening, or some other hobby. Regardless of whether it's a responsibility or a hobby, people enjoy learning about and succeeding at what they do. And it's fun and rewarding to get better at it!

The amount of time people spend trying to get better at something plays a huge role in whether or not they reach their goals. Like my Cowboy football players, the more time and effort people put into something, the more likely they are to earn and experience the positive payoffs that can come with achievement. It might be winning a competition, performing well under pressure, or any of the many ways people measure improvement and success. One thing I've found to be true for most everyone is that there's nothing better than the positive feelings that come from a job well done.

It's not rocket science to understand that the more time you put into something, the more likely you are to get better at it. And, your resolve to improve and succeed also is likely to get stronger. One of my former players, Ian, is a good illustration of this. Ian wasn't physically or athletically gifted. He was a big-framed kid who hadn't played much football. And one of his legs was a little shorter than the other, so he walked and ran with a limp. During his sophomore year at Boys Town High School, I remember telling one of my assistant coaches that if Ian had to play for us, we were in trouble.

Over the next couple of years, Ian worked hard at practice and put forth great effort in the weight room.

He was determined and enthusiastic, and over time, he got stronger and improved his coordination and athletic ability. His senior year, Ian started every football game for us and was one of our best offensive linemen. Ian is proof positive that time – along with blood, sweat, and tears – can cement a commitment to goals and achieving them.

While putting in the time it takes to pursue a goal is important, this, by itself, is still not enough. The time people put in must be well spent – in other words, it must be quality time. This is where a guide like a teacher, coach, or mentor can play a crucial role. You can be a tremendous asset to kids and, many times, a deciding factor in their success. Why? Because you have the experience and knowledge to help kids (like Ian) plan and use their time efficiently and effectively

The Three "F's"

My priorities in life revolve around what I like to call the three "F's": faith, family, and football. You probably understand why faith and family are on this list. But football? Let me explain. Every day for many years, I've worked hard to become, in my younger days, the best player, and later, the best coach, I could be.

During my playing days, I spent a great deal of time, both with the team and on my own, doing what it took to get better. As a coach, I commit a tremendous amount of time and energy to helping my players and team improve and succeed. I do the same with my family and faith; in these areas of my life, I invest a lot of time and effort.

Today, coaching football is my profession, and I love everything about it. For as long as I can remember, football has been in my blood and an integral part of my life. Because of the time and effort I've invested in football over the years, I've developed a total commitment to improving and succeeding, both as a player and now as a coach. All of this has taught me valuable lessons that I've applied to other aspects of my life. It's also given me a wealth of knowledge and experience that I feel is important to share with and teach to my students and players.

Put Your Money Where Your Mouth Is

I've found that the best way for me to begin teaching the lesson of commitment to kids is to use an analogy that involves something they all can relate to – money! I ask kids to imagine that they've taken all of their hard-earned money and invested every penny in the stock market. Then I ask them how much time they would spend improving their knowledge of business, researching and finding the best performing stocks, investing in the market, and tracking their investments. As you can imagine, the kids are always quick to say they'd be willing to spend a lot of time on those activities.

Next, I pose a different scenario to them. What if they invested only a very small portion of their money in the stock market? Then, how much time would they be willing to spend learning about business and stocks? You guessed right! Very little. They say they wouldn't care nearly as much if they lost or made money because the investment was so small. There's just not that much to lose or gain.

The kids and I then discuss how these two scenarios are the same for many things in life (relationships, school, sports, extracurricular activities, etc.). The more time, money, or effort they have invested in something, the more important it becomes. With a big or total investment, a person tries harder, success becomes more important, losing and/or failing hurts more, and a commitment is formed.

Up and At 'Em!

Commitment isn't about a time investment alone. Some of my players show up and go through drills and conditioning and still don't have a true and deep commitment to improving. They just go through the motions. To develop a *full* commitment to something, it's also important for young people to be mentally and emotionally invested.

I sometimes have a "Great Pretender" on my team. A Great Pretender is a player who shows up for practices and games with all his gear on and thinks that's all he needs to do to call himself a football player. I tell my players that commitment requires much more than just dressing for the part. I don't show up for work dressed like a policeman because I haven't invested the time it takes to become a policeman. You can help kids avoid being Great Pretenders by structuring your time with them so it's filled with productive and effective learning exercises, activities, and drills. This will teach them how to use time wisely and in ways that will help them build a true commitment to success.

One way I try to develop the necessary investment in my players is to get them involved in football-related activities year round. For example, during the summer, our players are required to condition in the weight room, work on position drills, and learn character lessons in the classroom five days a week, from 6:45 a.m. to 8 a.m. As you know, this is really early for kids (especially in the summertime!) to train and condition.

Could I hold these activities and practices at a later time in the day or get the players to accomplish what I want in a shorter period of time? Sure. But, I've found this type of "get-out-of-bed-and-get-going" schedule helps to create and strengthen that emotional and mental commitment to football.

Most players who make it through a full summer of these activities become fully committed to succeeding in football. Physically, they're in tip-top shape and ready to go for fall practice. Mentally and emotionally, they've become very attached to and invested in the team and program because they've successfully met these rigorous requirements. And, they want to continue improving as individual players and as a team.

When this commitment exists, it's harder for the players to quit or give up during preseason practices, in-season practices, and during games. Their resolve to improve and succeed is strengthened, and a passion, appreciation, and love for what they're doing is formed and established. When this happens, I've got a team full of players who are committed to common goals.

On the Same Page

When kids become totally and fully committed to an endeavor, it can lead to many great benefits for them and for you. Here are a few:

- **EVERYONE KNOWS WHO'S ONBOARD.** Young people eventually have to decide for themselves whether or not they're willing to do what it takes to reach goals and succeed. You can't do it for them. You are only their guide during the journey. When kids commit, everyone involved knows who wants to be there and who doesn't, and who wants to put in the work and who doesn't. In football, I want to hit the field on game day with players who are fully committed to success and winning. These are the players who will listen and respond to my coaching. They're the players who have the best shot at succeeding because they are willing to put in the time and be committed.

- **KIDS TAKE OWNERSHIP.** When people commit, kids included, they take ownership of what they're doing. As a football coach, one of my main goals is to help players move from being involved to being committed so they take ownership of the team. When this happens, players voluntarily take on more and more responsibility for getting things done right. They do the big and little things on their own, without me getting after them.

I try to cultivate and incorporate this with our football team during the summer with "iron man" drills. Every Wednesday, players compete in a series of demanding conditioning drills like flipping tractor tires down a course and other unconventional training activities. The players enjoy them because it's a change from the usual daily grind. Toward the end of the summer, we give the stopwatches and whistles to a couple of seniors who've demonstrated commitment and leadership and tell them to run the drills. They are in charge. The assistant coaches and I sit in the stands and observe how the seniors lead and how the other players respond to them. (If anything gets out of hand, we are there to address and take care of it.) It's our way of helping players take ownership while also promoting and teaching leadership.

For some adults, it's hard to give up control to young people because they're afraid or concerned that the kids might mess up and fail. Don't let this attitude impede progress in your learning setting! Instead, once you're confident that your youth are fully committed, gradually give them more responsibility and see what happens. If they respond positively, give them a bit more. If your kids drop the ball once in a while, that's okay. They must have the opportunity to fail, because without it, they don't have the opportunity to succeed! Accepting responsibility is a big part of growing up and taking ownership of one's life.

■ **COMMITMENT CAN CREATE LEADERSHIP.** The best team leader I ever had in football wasn't even my best player. And, he struggled in other areas of his life. Jason wasn't the best athlete, an "A" student, or a model citizen at home. He struggled to make the right choices, like many youngsters do. But Jason was fully committed to the success of the Cowboy football program, and he took being part of the team very seriously. Jason would direct the team in stretching exercises, lead the pack during tough drills, and talk with players who weren't giving maximum effort or were bringing the team down. Jason was willing to take a risk! Attempting to be a leader can be an uncertain proposition for anyone, especially kids. Why? Because others may not respond, and rejection and failure are very real possibilities. But Jason was willing to take the risk because he was so committed. I've found that the best leaders tend to be those people who have a passion and desire for what they do and are willing to stick out their necks in spite of the possible negative outcomes

A Winning Game Plan

As coaches, teachers, and mentors, we have wonderful opportunities every day to teach and reinforce to young people the skills of investing time and becoming committed. Let's go over some suggestions and ideas that can help you make a plan for effectively teaching your kids these skills.

- **MAKE A SCHEDULE.** Create a detailed calendar that lists all the commitments you expect kids to make and follow through on. Include dates, starting and ending times, locations where activities will take place, and descriptions of what the kids will be doing and trying to accomplish. This way, everyone is on the same page and knows exactly what to do and expect.

There's an old axiom that says, "Eighty percent of success is showing up." Many adults who work with youth get upset and frustrated when they show up late or not at all. They might label kids "lazy," "irresponsible," or "unmotivated." These are harsh words to slap on any youngster. And many times, these labels are inaccurate. Why? Because many young people haven't been taught how to be on time or why it's important. Don't take anything for granted when it comes to teaching kids skills on managing time, even showing up on time to a commitment. Heck, it's a skill many adults struggle with! And it's something kids need to learn because it's the first step in creating a deep and full commitment to any endeavor. So, be prepared to teach youngsters why it's important to be on time and how to do it. Commitment begins with arriving on time and being prepared and ready to go.

- **MAKE IT QUALITY TIME.** To make your time with young people as productive and effective as possible, spend time in advance planning exactly what you want them to learn and how you'll go about teaching it. Doing this allows you to get the most out of your instruction time, gives kids a better opportunity to learn, and creates an efficient learning setting.

- **WRITE IT ALL DOWN.** In football, I have "practice plans" that spell out in detail what's going to happen during every minute of every practice, from drills to water breaks to talking strategy. I give the plans to all my assistant coaches prior to practices. We run a tight ship and value every minute we have to help our players learn. This makes our practices fast-paced and very organized – the kind of environment where good learning can occur. Do the same thing in your learning environment. Put it all on paper and stick to the plan.

- **INVOLVE KIDS.** When appropriate, and when kids have shown they're ready, allow them to have some input into how they will spend their learning time with you. For example, a fellow football coach uses a "Wheel of Fortune" during conditioning. Every now and then, he'll allow players to spin the wheel to determine what conditioning drill they will start off with that day. (The wheel also includes a "free day" slot on it, and if it lands there, the players get the day off from conditioning.) This is a great way to involve young people in their learning, and they have a blast with it! I'm not suggesting that you allow kids to determine content – that's your job and your responsibility. Rather, find creative ways that let youngsters make appropriate choices about lessons, activities, or drills.

- **CATCH 'EM BEING GOOD!** I can't emphasize this suggestion enough! Always be looking for opportunities to praise the kids who are investing time, giving effort, and working toward being fully committed. Kids love it when you pat them on the back or give them words of encouragement. Use a positive teaching approach and interaction style in your learning setting. When you do, you'll find that young people will continue to work hard so they can hear the good words from you again and again. As other kids see what it takes to earn your praise, they'll begin to put forth the right kind of effort and commitment. Trust me, praise is contagious!

- **USE REWARDS.** Be creative and find ways to reinforce hard work and commitment through recognition and rewards that work well for girls and boys in your learning setting. Most rewards cost little or no money, and praise is free. And believe me, they both work! You'll be amazed at the kind of effort kids will put forth for the opportunity to earn your praise or a reward. (Chapter 9, "Everyone Counts," goes into more detail about this strategy.)

■ **DESCRIBE THE BIGGER PICTURE.** Discuss with youngsters how the time investment, commitment, and effort they make in your particular learning setting carries over to other parts of their lives. Help them make the connection between what happens now and what happens in the outside world and in the future. For example, during early morning summer practices, I'll spend time talking to our players about how being able to get up early and make it to practice on time will help them when they have a job. Granted, the kids might not want to hear this at 6:30 in the morning. But it's my responsibility to have these kinds of conversations with my players and students. It might not sink in right there and then, but at least the seed has been planted.

■ **BE A ROLE MODEL.** Demonstrate for kids what time investment, hard work, and commitment are all about. They'll learn more from your actions than your words. I know this is true because players tell me they notice my car in the parking lot on the weekend or late at night during the postseason when I'm preparing a plan for a game. When the players see my level of commitment to the team and how much time I invest in helping them to get better and succeed, they begin to give a better effort themselves. Remember that kids are always watching and learning from what you do and say.

■ **ENJOY THE RIDE.** When your time with your kids comes to an end, make sure you acknowledge the growth that's taken place and all that's been achieved. I like to say every year in football that we "shoot for the moon," but most seasons "land in the stars." Only one team can win its last game in the playoffs and be state champion, but not winning the state championship doesn't mean my team failed. It's not all about winning. Instead, it's about getting young people to invest and commit themselves to goals and success. Most times, this is a huge accomplishment in and of itself. So, make sure you enjoy all that you and the kids accomplish together!

 Huddle Up!

Commitment comes from time and effort spent striving to realize goals. This was a lesson my Cowboy football players had yet to experience and learn. However, once they began committing more and more time and energy toward doing the right things they needed to do to improve, their resolve strengthened and they got better. Also, they moved from *being involved* to *being committed*. Once people are committed to achieve and succeed, there's not a lot that can stop them!

LEAVE NO STONE UNTURNED
Strategy: Be Prepared

"People perform most reliably when they're sure they can handle the task at hand, and that sureness comes with specific preparation."

– BILL PARCELLS
Coached the New York Giants to two Super Bowl victories

My second season as head football coach at Boys Town High School, we had a great year and qualified for the state playoffs for the first time in seven years. It was an exciting and uplifting time for the players and everyone on campus. In our first playoff game, we came from behind to

115

win. Our second-round game was against Valley High School on their home field – always a tough place to play. It was a close and hard-fought contest. With less than a minute to go in the game, Valley scored and cut our lead to four points. I knew what was coming next, and I also knew that my players weren't going to be ready for it. We had yet to introduce to our players and have them practice how to receive an onside kick. Throughout the year, there had been so many basic things we had to teach that this kind of unique situation went completely under the radar. During the little time I had before the kickoff, I tried to quickly identify the "good hands" players (those kids who were used to catching and touching the football). They huddled around me and I quickly explained what was about to happen, how they were to line up, and what the players should do. Basically, I was coaching on the fly something we should have already practiced many times. Not all my players understood where to go and what to do, and I could see unease and confusion on some faces, which is typical when people are unprepared.

The onside kick ricocheted off one of my player's hands and was recovered by Valley. This shifted the momentum of the game dramatically, and Valley was brimming with hope and confidence. Just a few minutes earlier, it looked like we had the game well in hand. Now, we were back on our heels, reeling from the sudden change. Valley drove down the field and got inside our five-yard line. On the last play of the game, our defense dug in and came up big with a goal-line stand to preserve the victory.

The following day, the very first thing I did was start preparing my "hands" kickoff return team. I got out a piece of paper and identified all the players who would be on this particular team. Next, I drew up the alignment, put players in the spots that would best suit them and the unit, and wrote out what each player's responsibilities were in various situations. I blended all this into the practice plan, and we worked on it first thing that day during practice. We rehearsed onside kicks until the coaches and players were comfortable with how it all worked. And we continued to practice it every day that week. To this day, we still spend a portion of practice every week going over this unique situation.

■ ■ ■

As a young head coach, I didn't have my team prepared and it almost cost us an important game. It was a detail that got lost in the hustle and bustle of focusing on teaching my players and team the basic skills that come into play more often during games. However, this was no excuse for not having my players prepared, because onside kicks can be significant plays in football. It's my job to have my players and team prepared for every situation. Many times, we learn best from our mistakes and this was certainly true for me in this situation.

Working with young people in any environment can be challenging. Not only do you have to prepare and teach the content and skills that apply to your specific learning setting, but you also have to be ready for the many behaviors – especially the unexpected and negative ones – that often enter into the equation and affect teaching and learning.

Some days everything runs smoothly. Other days, a kid may be upset due to something totally unrelated to your learning environment (e.g., a problem at home or with a friend), and everything you wanted to accomplish that day can go completely out the window. That's why it's important for you to carefully plan the things you have control over, like lesson and practice plans. That way, when a curveball comes your way, you'll be better able to handle it competently and with confidence. And once the hurdle has been cleared, you can smoothly transition back to your teaching.

Do What You Signed Up to Do

I define being prepared very simply. It's doing the job you were hired or chose to do with kids – whether as a teacher, coach, parent, mentor, or volunteer. Whatever your role, one of your top responsibilities is to work hard to be the best you can be. This means paying attention to the details and taking the time to plan, learn, and improve your skills in all areas of your learning setting.

There are many benefits to being prepared for both you and your youth. Being prepared:

- **BUILDS CONFIDENCE.** Being prepared helps adults feel more competent in their teaching and in their ability to deal with the unexpected, like behavior issues. Kids know what's expected of them and what's acceptable regarding performance and behavior.

- **TEACHES IMPORTANT LIFE SKILLS.** Modeling and teaching youngsters how to effectively plan and organize helps them learn how to achieve goals and be successful, both in your learning setting and in other aspects of their lives.

- **CREATES A BETTER LEARNING ENVIRONMENT.** Planning and organization enhances teaching and learning. Being prepared cuts down on disruptions and lets you and your kids make the most of every teachable moment.

- **LETS EVERYONE KNOW WHO'S IN CHARGE.** The kids know you're in control of what happens in the learning setting, from determining content to setting behavioral expectations. A disorganized learning setting can quickly become chaotic and lead to behavior problems. When you are prepared and in command, kids will be more willing to put their trust in you.

- **EASES ADULT FRUSTRATION AND ANXIETY LEVELS.** Being prepared in the areas you can control provides some comfort and ease of mind when things do get hectic and stressful with the kids (and they will!).

- **ALLOWS FOR THE DEVELOPMENT OF A FUN AND REWARDING LEARNING ENVIRONMENT.** When your teaching is effective and young people are learning, the result can be good relationships between you and the kids. Learning becomes a give-and-take process, and you and the kids look forward to being together and working together.

- **ALLOWS YOU TO BE MORE ENERGETIC AND ENTHUSED.** And this kind of attitude rubs off on the girls and boys!

If You Fail to Plan, You Plan to Fail

Planning, being organized, and paying attention to details is the only way to remain poised, secure, and strong in what you're teaching, how you're teaching it, and how you're running your learning environment. When it comes to teaching and learning, being prepared contributes mightily to successful outcomes. It also allows you to handle the uncertainties and unpredictability of life with young people. When kids bring outside problems into your learning setting, or when issues arise in your personal life, or when difficulties arise within your learning community, having a plan will make it easier to deal with these situations. I'm not saying a plan will solve every possible problem, but not having one will make matters worse.

Life is filled with moments we can't plan for. But you can learn to handle these times so much better – without frustration, irritation, and upset – when you plan and prepare well in the areas you can control, like content, rules, behavioral expectations, and others.

Let's go over some specific ideas and suggestions for being better prepared in your learning setting.

- **DETERMINE LONG-TERM, INTERMEDIATE, AND SHORT-TERM GOALS.** Then, decide what daily and weekly tasks must be performed and/or mastered to reach these goals. (See Chapter 3, "First and Goal," for specific information on goal-setting.) Next, write everything down in an easy-to-refer-to format and set a realistic time frame for successfully attaining these goals. Finally, share all this with the kids. With some groups of kids, it's a good idea to get their input during each stage. This helps them take some ownership and responsibility, and creates a firmer commitment to success. It also reinforces the importance of being prepared.

- **"WORKING HARD" AND "BEING PREPARED" AREN'T THE SAME THING.** Many youth think that spending lots of time doing something is good preparation and will automatically result in success. For example, a student might spend hours studying for a test but still fail because he or she didn't study the right things or study in a productive way. Kids often confuse being "busy" with using their time effectively and efficiently. When you are properly prepared to teach and your kids are properly prepared to learn, you make the most of your time together and get more accomplished. It's all about making good use of the time you do have. For example, my assistant coaches and I plan out and value every minute of football practice. We keep the players moving from drill to drill and don't quit any of the drills early. We make the most of each and every minute so that the entire time we're together is used to its fullest potential. Do the same in your learning setting. Focus on maximizing the time you spend teaching kids and modeling for them how to use time wisely.

- **Don't assume!** Many times, adults take for granted that young people know how to be prepared or get prepared. Being prepared is one of the first skills I teach my students at the beginning of each year. I teach them that in order to be prepared for class, they need to have a pencil with an eraser, paper, a notebook, a calculator, and a textbook. And, I'll even give them a minute to get everything out so they're ready to learn. My point here is that you must tell your kids exactly what it means to be prepared in your learning setting. This also applies to basic social skills like following instructions, accepting feedback, accepting consequences, and others. Don't assume that all kids know how to line up properly, or how to behave appropriately when they disagree with you about a test grade or a negative consequence they've earned. You should teach (or at least review) these skills to all your girls and boys. It sets the tone for how you expect them to be prepared in the future.

- **BREAK DOWN THE DISCIPLINES OF YOUR SUBJECT MATTER INTO THEIR SIMPLEST FORMS.** Begin by preparing and teaching kids the basics or fundamentals. Once these have been mastered, you can move to more complex content, skills, and drills. Prepare your lessons or drills so that youngsters can digest information in manageable pieces. This will allow your teaching to build on itself, which results in better outcomes for learning. For example, many adults fail to recognize that successfully completing homework is a skill, and that it requires layers of teaching. For one of your students, the first step (or most fundamental task) of this skill might be teaching him or her how to accurately write down homework assignments in an assignment notebook. Next, you might have to teach the child how to prioritize what to study. If he or she wants to work on an art project that's due in two weeks, but there's an algebra test the next day, you have to teach the child that studying for the test comes first. Then if time permits, he or she can work on the art project. There are more complex study skills that you can teach once students have mastered the fundamentals. Also, remember that kids have a wide range of abilities, and they learn and comprehend at different rates. This means planning and preparing your teaching so everyone can understand it.

■ **REVIEW AND TEST WHAT YOU'RE TEACHING AND WHAT YOU'RE ASKING YOUNG PEOPLE TO DO.** Put yourself in their shoes to determine if what you're teaching is too hard – or too easy. You want to make sure the kids understand your teaching methods and the outcomes you expect from them are realistic and doable. For example, before I teach my quarterbacks new footwork for the passing or running game, I spend time actually doing the footwork myself. If it's difficult for me to do, then my quarterbacks are probably not going to be able to do it well either. That's when I head back to the drawing board to revise my preparation by breaking down skills and drills into even simpler steps. And, I might need to adjust my coaching and teaching or change my expectations for how long it might take my players to master the footwork. In the end, I might decide that what I'm asking is too complex for my players to perform. Then, I have to modify my expectations or possibly even scrap what I wanted to do and start over. One other thing I've found to be helpful: If you're having trouble with all this, test what you want to teach kids on another adult. A peer can offer a wealth of knowledge and provide you with great feedback, advice, and suggestions on how to get things accomplished more effectively and efficiently.

■ **PLAN YOUR ATTACK AND ATTACK YOUR PLAN.**
Once your lesson or practice plan is developed
and ready to go, write it all down and stick to it.
Be specific and detailed with everything you do
and want to accomplish. I prepare by scripting
every play we run in practice. That way, all my
assistant coaches are fully prepared to evaluate
and teach, and our practices run more smoothly
and crisply. We get a lot of valuable teaching
done in the short amount of time we have.
Preparation like this helps maximize the number
of repetitions players get to do, which can result
in better and quicker learning.

■ **ADJUST YOUR PREPARATION AND PLANS BASED
ON THE KIDS' PERFORMANCE.** Always evaluate
how youngsters are doing and remain flexible
and open to change if they are struggling or
can't grasp what's being taught. Have a "contingency plan" just in case things go a bit haywire.
In all my game plans, I strategize for and develop adjustments we can turn to if what we've
planned to do doesn't go as expected. I rarely
use these contingency plans, but I know they
are there if I need them. And it's much easier to
adjust to sudden change when you're prepared
for it.

■ **DON'T GO OVERBOARD WITH YOUR PREPARATION.**
While it's important to cover all the bases in
your preparation, getting caught up in too many

details or issues can lead to "paralysis by analysis." Avoid polluting and complicating things by thinking too much or letting too many details overwhelm you. Let's face it, if you're struggling to decide what you want to do and how you're going to teach it, the kids will never learn a thing. Remember the acronym KISS – "Keep It Simple Stupid!"

Huddle Up!

When your preparation is good, success is more likely to come to you and your kids. This means you must be willing to put in the time to determine the most appropriate content to teach, along with how to go about teaching it in ways that are efficient, effective, and best suited for your kids and your learning environment. Once that's done (which is no easy feat!), remain flexible and open to possible adjustments and changes.

Planning is time-consuming and requires hard work; it's not for the weak of heart. If you really want to succeed, and help your kids succeed too, you've got to properly prepare. Working toward and reaching goals is a journey that requires effort and sacrifice, but it doesn't have to be one filled with pain or misery. A good plan of action helps make the journey more enjoyable and the road traveled smoother and straighter.

EVERYONE COUNTS
Strategy: Catch 'Em Being Good

"He was the only one of us who didn't get on the ice in the Olympic tournament, but he was a great influence on me and he busted his butt for us and I want to thank him publicly for making me a better person."

– JIM CRAIG
*Goalie for the 1980 gold medal U.S. Olympic hockey team,
speaking about Steve Janaszak, the USA's backup goalie*

At the beginning of the summer a number of years ago, Charles came to me and said he'd like to try out for the football team. He wasn't a big kid and he had little football experience. From the beginning, Charles knew he probably wasn't going to be a starter or even get much playing time. But he wanted to be part of the team, and he believed he could contribute in some way. He had a great attitude and an even better work ethic. During summer conditioning and spring practices, he outworked many of the kids who would start or see a lion's share of playing time. Charles encouraged and pushed other players by conditioning and practicing with intensity and a commitment to doing things the right way. Charles's effort in the weight room and on the practice field helped set the tone and expectations for the rest of the team.

During the regular season, we give out a "Scout Team" award before each game. The award isn't for the starters or players who will see lots of action in the game. Instead, it's reserved for players like Charles who've worked hard all week in practice to help prepare the starters for the game. The player who earns the award is an honorary captain for that week's game and carries the Cowboy flag while leading the team onto the field before the game. He also represents the team, along with the other captains, for the coin toss. Our scout team players value this award and work hard to get it, and the starters respect those who earn it.

During that particular year, Charles earned the Scout Team award more weeks than any other player on the team. He took immense pride in being a scout team member and working behind the scenes to help our team succeed. Charles discovered a role on the team that allowed him to contribute in a big way. On top of giving out the Scout Team award, my assistant coaches and I praised and recognized Charles (and others like him) as often as possible for his positive attitude and contributions.

After graduating from Boys Town High School, Charles spent a year at a college prep school working on his grades. The next year, he applied to and was accepted at West Point Military Academy, one of the most prestigious and challenging colleges in the United States. Charles showed me and others that everyone has a unique gift and a role to play that can allow him or her to contribute and succeed.

■ ■ ■

Charles and Steve Janaszak (the backup goalie for the 1980 U.S. Olympic hockey team) weren't the top players on their teams. But they found and developed roles that allowed them to be essential contributors. Both supported, encouraged, and pushed those who would play more to become better, and they toiled every day to help prepare the team to achieve success. And, they did all this knowing their efforts would likely go unnoticed and unrecognized by almost everyone outside the team.

Unselfish players and students like these two don't come along very often, and when they do, it's a joy to be around them. Their positive attitude, zest, and appreciation for "being a part of" is infectious. It makes me strive to be a better coach and teacher, and pushes others to work harder and become more committed.

I tell my students and players that everyone is a champion at something because God doesn't make garbage. Garbage has no "nutritional value" and can lead to sickness and disease. When kids think and believe they have no nutritional value – or nothing to offer – this too can lead to illness and disease, like depression, anxiety, behavior disorders, and more.

Every youngster has value and something to offer. I challenge and help students and players to discover their special gifts by asking them what they can bring to the table. It might be a good sense of humor, the ability to laugh at themselves, showing up on time and not complaining, or being a good listener. Gifts and talents are varied and limitless – and everyone has at least one, and likely, many.

As a coach, teacher, or mentor, your job is to help young people recognize that they have value, unique talents, and special gifts to offer others and the world around them. Once uncovered, you help cultivate these talents through encouragement, praise, and rewards so kids are willing to share their gifts with you and others. All this helps make your learning setting a positive one where youngsters can grow, thrive, and achieve.

Opening Doors

When you're the adult in charge of kids and their learning, you have many responsibilities. One of the most important of these is to open doors of opportunity for the young people in your particular setting. It's up to you to do your best to teach kids how to play the guitar, become an Eagle Scout, be a volleyball player, reduce fractions, or whatever it is you are teaching. Opening doors simply means providing youth with the knowledge and skills they need for success and explaining how to best use them, both in your setting and in others.

As a coach and teacher, I work hard to help kids recognize doors of opportunity and to learn how to walk through them. However, I know I can't force youngsters to go through the doors. It's an individual choice each girl and boy has to make. Unfortunately, some kids fail to recognize an opportunity and others choose to turn around and walk away. But I've found that most take hold of opportunity with enthusiasm and action. Our job is simply to prepare them for these opportunities by giving them the tools they need to succeed.

Every young person you work with has an opportunity to learn and benefit from your teaching. Some kids might gain more from your time together than others, but they all gain something. For example, we all have kids who struggle with the content we're trying to teach them. With these kids, our interactions with them might be the most important lesson. They might learn from your encouragement and praise that they do in fact have value and are capable of achieving. And that's a huge lesson for kids to learn!

Keep Slinging Mud

One of the hardest things for teachers, coaches, and mentors is seeing a child not take advantage of an opportunity. It can be frustrating and disheartening. However, it's important to remain upbeat and optimistic with all your kids and to continue your efforts no matter what certain kids choose to do. All you can do is "keep slinging mud" – have faith, go on with your teaching, and hope that eventually something will "stick."

Antonio came out for our football team his sophomore year. He had plenty of potential but didn't work hard in practice or in the weight room. He had a negative attitude and was a hard kid to like. Over time, we continued to encourage Antonio to put forth his best effort. My assistant coaches and I refused to give up on him. One day, I spoke with Antonio and asked him to concentrate on giving a good effort in the weight room. That was all – just work hard at getting stronger. I began to work with him one-on-one, all the while encouraging him to get after it.

Antonio, like all our players, charted his progress and began to see he was getting stronger and stronger. He started lifting more on his own time. Soon, he just "took off" to a point where he was self-motivated to improve. Two years later, he and a few other seniors came up to me with a list of players who were not having a positive impact on the team or hustling – guys who were loafing and bringing the team down. What a transformation in Antonio! He went from a reluctant and unenthusiastic participant to a full-fledged and committed team leader.

Keep in mind that youngsters realize the benefits you and your teaching provide at their own pace, not yours. You have to be patient with kids and diligent in your teaching, and come to an understanding that you may never see the fruits of your labor. It might be well on down the road when your influence and teaching has its greatest impact on a young person's life.

For many kids, it takes time and perspective before they "get it" and realize that you actually know what you're talking about. So, keep slinging mud! You're planting seeds for the future, seeds that might have to lay dormant for a while before they begin to take root and show signs of life.

Move the Sticks

We all need help along the way. This is especially true for youngsters, when learning is new, sometimes difficult, and often painful. Some kids just need booster shots of encouragement, praise, and pats on the back to keep them moving forward. Others, however, need much more. With these kids, more formal kinds of reinforcement and structured rewards are needed to keep them motivated and on the right path.

A good example of a formal reward is the Scout Team award I mentioned at the beginning of this chapter. Another reward I use with my football players is the Eagle award. We give out this award after every game. It goes to the player who "soared like an eagle" – hustled, made big plays, and gave the greatest effort – the entire game. The player who wins this award receives a statue of an eagle to keep for one week. It always amazes me how much it means to the players to get to keep this old, beat-up statue for seven days. But, it's an honor that represents effort and commitment, two characteristics that our players and coaches hold in high regard.

The Scout Team and Eagle awards are structured rewards created for different kinds of players on the team. One is geared toward kids who won't play in games but are crucial to our preparation, while the other encourages our starters to give maximum effort during games. Even though they are designed for different groups, they both have the same purpose and goal: to motivate all players on the team to continue to improve and succeed.

These awards work well to help motivate and encourage kids to learn and achieve on the football field. In the classroom, you can create similar rewards and awards for daily participation, monthly attendance, outstanding effort, good behavior, or anything else you want to see more often or done better. Whatever your setting, look for effective and creative ways to keep your kids interested in learning. When praise and rewards are in place and used regularly, you'll find that your learning setting is a much more positive and nurturing environment – one where youth enjoy working hard to achieve. In addition, kids will view you as being fair and concerned about them, which helps create better relationships.

So, examine your learning setting and determine what makes your kids tick. Look for ways to motivate them so learning and achieving continue to be their goals. Never give up on young people just because they're struggling with content or because their behavior isn't up to par. Instead, persevere and determine how you can best guide them to and through the doors of opportunity.

A Winning Game Plan

Hinges hold doors securely in place and allow them to be opened and closed. Every door of opportunity has hinges so it can open and stay open. The following suggestions and ideas are what I like to think of as the hinges that help keep doors of opportunity open for kids to walk through.

- **STRUCTURE.** Lack of organization and structure in your learning setting can result in confusion and even chaos. When this happens, learning is disrupted and kids fail. So, it's up to you to put a system in place that provides structure and stability in your setting. The main building block for doing this involves setting expectations that are clear and attainable. (See Chapter 1, "First and Ten.") Here, you develop and determine performance and behavior expectations for your girls and boys. Then you discuss these expectations with them so no one is left guessing. These expectations become the road map for success because they spell out exactly the way things are to be done in your setting.

- **DISCIPLINE.** Once your structure is in place, you have to make sure kids adhere to it. The way to maintain structure in your setting is by using

135

consequences – both positive and negative. I've found that really good teachers, coaches, and mentors rely heavily on giving praise, positive reinforcement, and positive consequences for appropriate behaviors. At Girls and Boys Town, we follow the "4-to-1 rule" with our kids. This means for every negative consequence or correction a youth earns for inappropriate behavior, we look for at least four opportunities to praise and reinforce the youth for using a positive behavior. With some kids, the ratio can be as high as 8 to 1 or 10 to 1; it all depends on the youth and his or her individual needs. For example, at football practice, I might say something like this to a receiver who just dropped a pass: "Good explosion off the line of scrimmage (praise) and you ran a great route (praise). I liked the way you lowered your center of gravity when you broke out of your route (praise), and you kept your elbows in (praise). Next time, have big eyes and follow the ball into your hands (correction)."

Our motto is "Catch'em being good!" For many adults, this kind of approach doesn't come naturally and is sometimes difficult to adopt. Why? Because many people simply expect kids to be able to do the right thing and make good choices. They believe youngsters should be doing these things anyway, and since it all should come naturally, why praise them? Well, trust me, it doesn't come naturally! Kids struggle just like everybody else (young and old) to do the next right thing and make sound decisions. Looking for positive behaviors to praise doesn't mean you ignore negative behavior; you still continue to address negative behaviors by teaching alternative positive behaviors and giving negative consequences. But you're always on the lookout for the good stuff kids do. Praising and reinforcing young people when they take the right action and/or make good decisions motivates them to repeat those positive behaviors and lets them know you notice when they do. Praise, reinforcement, and positive consequences are keys to helping kids feel confident about themselves and their ability to succeed.

- **FEEDBACK**. Giving feedback or criticism to youngsters is a crucial part of the teaching and learning process. It's really where learning takes place. When you use lots of praise and reinforcement, kids are much more likely to respond positively to your feedback. When you ride or harp on them all the time, kids get frustrated and upset, and eventually they shut out you and your teaching. So, make sure you're using lots of praise with youth in your setting. Then, when they mess up and need feedback and correction, start off with praise or empathy. For example, if a player doesn't execute his assignment at football practice, I might start with praise by saying something like, "Good hustle out there! Now, let's look at exactly what you're supposed to do." Or, I might use empathy and say, "I know you're getting tired, but let's go over what your assignment is again."

Another way to give feedback so that kids will respond more positively is to remind them about the ultimate goal. I might say something like, "In order to be the starting quarterback, you have to be able to execute this play. So let's go over it again." All three ways start your teaching in a positive manner, taking the sting out of feedback and making it easier for kids to be open to your correction and teaching.

■ **PRETEACH.** Most young people tend to take criticism personally. If that leads to an emotional response, it can disrupt learning and harm your relationship with kids. One easy way to deal with these issues is to take time upfront to explain to youngsters how the teaching and learning process works. Let them know that mistakes and setbacks will happen; it's an inevitable part of the learning process. People rarely learn on the first try or even the second or third. Sometimes, it might take a long time for your teaching to sink in and make sense to kids. Let them know that's okay and that everyone learns at his or her own pace. Also let them know that you will praise and/or reinforce them when they do things correctly, and will correct them through feedback when they make mistakes. Your job is to help young people do things the right way so they are prepared and capable of walking through the doors of opportunity. Talking with kids beforehand – what we call preteaching – about how teaching and criticism go hand-in-hand in the learning process helps them understand that it's nothing personal and that you really care about them and their ability to succeed.

■ **A BALANCING ACT.** Every teacher, coach, and mentor has strengths and weaknesses when it comes to relationships and discipline with young people. Some adults are really good at establishing healthy relationships pretty quickly with kids, but aren't as strong when it comes to creating structure and using discipline and consequences. Others, however, are able to create a structured, organized setting and teach to performance and behavior problems without much of a struggle. But they might have problems building relationships with kids. It's normal to be strong in one area and weak in the other. The goal is to strike a balance between your relationship and discipline skills. To do that, you first have to become aware of your strengths and weaknesses, then you can focus and work on improving them. Finding a balance means having good relationships with kids, where you trust and respect each other, and still being able to discipline them when needed. Structure, discipline, and consequences should not be so overbearing that girls and boys feel stifled, uptight, or hesitant to express themselves and how they feel. It's a delicate balance that ebbs and flows, and one that you need to constantly monitor and adjust.

Huddle Up!

Young people come to your learning setting with a grocery sack of their own gifts and talents. It's your job to help them sort through the sack and figure out what's good and fresh that will nourish them on their journey. You also have to point out to kids what needs to be tossed out because it has no nutritional value. Remember: All children have talents and value; all they need is a person like you to bring out their best.

Looking back, we all can remember a teacher, coach, or mentor who stood by us through thick and thin and who continued to encourage us no matter what. This is what you are called to do with each and every youngster in your learning setting. Yes, it's a real challenge with some kids. But there's no better feeling of satisfaction than seeing kids open the door of opportunity and step across the threshold.

BREAD AND BUTTER
Strategy: Practice the Fundamentals

"First, master the fundamentals."

– LARRY BIRD
*12-time NBA All-Star who led the
Boston Celtics to three NBA Championships*

We have a period during football practice called "bread and butter." This time involves players moving from station to station doing different drills. Some stations and drills are specifically designed for skill players, while others are designed for linemen. The drills help teach each group of players three basic skills they need to master in order to be good at their positions. Even though the stations and drills are different for various players, the ultimate goal is the same: to teach players the fundamental skills of their positions and to practice these skills over and over until they become second nature. During the bread and butter period, we "rep the fundamentals." This means all the players do repetition after repetition of the same drills so they can hone and perfect the three basic skills they need to succeed.

Many times, coaches say their teams need to get "back to the basics." This usually happens following a loss or poor performance. My coaching philosophy is that you should never leave the fundamentals. They should be taught and practiced over and over from the beginning of the season to the end – and during the off-season, if possible. This is the only way effective learning can occur and skills can stick with kids.

Early on, during summer and preseason practices, we run bread and butter periods every single day. It's the majority of what we do at practice this time of the year. As the season progresses, we spend less time and have fewer practices with bread and butter drills. By year's end, we only have them a couple of times a week. But even though we spend less time and fewer practices going over the basics, we never fully stop working on them.

Once players master the basic skills of their positions, we're able to move on to higher-level skills and techniques and more complex formations and schemes. Without mastering the fundamentals, however, higher-level teaching and learning is virtually impossible. The basic skills are the foundation of everything we teach our players and team. For our foundation to be rock solid, the fundamental skills have to be taught and mastered. Otherwise, everything can come tumbling down in an instant.

■ ■ ■

Many kids come to me poorly prepared for high school football. They might know where to start off and where to go on offense and defense, but they don't know how to *do* football fundamentals properly and safely. So I have to start over and work with them on the basics.

At the many youth football practices I've attended over the years, I've observed that most youth coaches have good intentions, but sometimes lose focus of the right things. For example, many start their players out with some light stretching, followed by a few drills to help teach fundamental skills. Then, the majority of practice is spent throwing bombs, running complicated plays like reverses and flea flickers, and live scrimmaging. Other coaches just get bored spending most of their practice going over the same drills again and again. Heck, they're coaches and they're eager to get to the sophisticated and intricate stuff.

But, few young players can comprehend the complicated plays that are being taught, and they aren't physically developed enough to do these more advanced activities competently or successfully. What these players really need is to "rep the fundamentals." They need to learn and practice – over and over – the basic skills of football (e.g., blocking, tackling, and holding on to the football) in order to build a solid foundation.

Today, winning seems to be the main goal in youth sports. This often interferes with proper coaching and prevents kids from developing good playing skills. When coaching younger players, the main goal should be simple: teach them basic skills so they have a solid base for future and more advanced learning. Winning should be way down on the list of priorities.

No matter the learning setting, it's important to start with the fundamentals. It's the best way for kids to learn and succeed.

Building Blocks

All disciplines (academics, sports, music, Scouting, etc.) have basic building blocks that provide the foundation, or starting place, for everything else. Good teaching and successful learning starts with these basic elements. Skipping them or moving too fast sets up young people for poor performance and, ultimately, failure. For example, in offensive football, it's fruitless to run complicated plays with elaborate formations if the skill players (quarterbacks, running backs, and receivers) can't hold on to the ball. To run any offense, a team has to have the football and keep it. That's why we first teach our skill players ball security – or how to correctly carry or hold the football so the defense can't strip it away. And players practice this through drills and many, many repetitions. Only after this skill is mastered do we move on to other things.

The formula for successful and long-lasting learning is really pretty simple. It's about building a strong foundation by first teaching basic elements and reinforcing them through repetition. So always start your teaching at the beginning with the basic building blocks. Once youngsters are competent in the basic skills, you can move on to introducing intermediate and advanced elements and skills. Successful learning is based on this simple formula. And good coaches, teachers, and mentors believe in it and stick to it.

This learning formula is beneficial to you and the kids in many ways:

- Youth learn they can't cut corners, and that there are no shortcuts to success.

- Kids discover that in the learning process, there is a sequential pattern to learning and they can't skip a step or move ahead until the previous step is mastered.

- Adults can identify areas where youngsters are deficient and require more teaching.

- When young people practice the fundamentals over and over, they develop confidence in what they can do, and believe they can succeed when the real thing happens. For example, at the beginning of each season, kids new to football are timid when it comes to hitting and tackling. They're afraid it will hurt or that they will get hurt. That's why we spend a great deal of time breaking down proper tackling techniques into smaller components (e.g., head, shoulder, and hand position; footwork) that players can understand and do.

And we practice these over and over. This may go on for many days before players are allowed to do any live tackling. We want them prepared and confident in how to tackle properly and safely. The learning process can be slow, but by the time it's over, the fear has faded, confidence has risen, and players are itching to hit!

- The final product is polished and looks effortless. How many times have you heard it said that the reason one team won was because they were "fundamentally sound"? Lots! It may sound like a cliché, but it's really true!

- Students learn more quickly and retain what they learn longer.

- Mastering the fundamentals prepares kids for the many curveballs that will inevitably come their way.

- Performance and outcomes improve. Kids get better and they succeed!

Maximize Your Time

Very few young people are smart or talented enough to learn and master something the first time around – or even the second or third. Most kids require many, many learning trials before it sinks in. And it takes even more time before they become really proficient at a task or an endeavor.

A big part of your job is to maximize the time you have to "rep the fundamentals" with youth in your learning setting. One way to do this is to "teach on the run." This means giving kids feedback and correction on their performance as they do the skill(s), then quickly moving to another repetition. That way, feedback on how to improve is fresh and youngsters are more likely to correct their performance and do it right during the next repetition.

We "coach on the run" all the time during football practices. Coaches continually provide praise and feedback to their position players as they run back to the huddle to repeat a play or head back to a line to go over a drill again. We rarely stop the flow of practice to spend a long time talking to a player or players about performance. Instead, we focus on teaching and "repping the fundamentals" as much as possible in the time we have.

You can do the same thing in your learning setting. Look for ways to practice the basics of your discipline as many times as possible. However, make sure you're always providing quality feedback. Keep your teaching at a brisk pace, but not so fast that you lose kids. You'll always have some girls and boys who lag behind and struggle for various reasons. Be sure to spend time with these kids after class or help them practice skills during extra one-on-one teaching. Every teacher, coach, and mentor would love to have more teaching time, but it's just not always possible. So use the time you do have wisely and efficiently.

A Winning Game Plan

Helping young people learn is a challenge, especially when they are starting out with something new. One important component that helps make learning easier and teaching more effective is for you to break down the large concepts into smaller, more manageable pieces. Give it to kids in little bites that are within their capabilities and that they can understand.

In this section, I'm going to describe to you how I break down concepts into basic skills. I've successfully used this process in the classroom and on the playing field.

- **IDENTIFY SKILLS.** First, determine the basic skills kids need to learn to be successful in your discipline. With my football team, I do a thorough analysis of every position on the team. For each position, I identify the basic skills players need to learn. Until this analysis is complete, I don't draw up one new play or even develop a practice plan. My first job is to make sure my players know what to do and learn the basics of their positions. Once I determine the fundamental skills my kids need, I write them down so there's a tangible list of what my coaches and I need to teach players.

  There are many ways to identify the fundamental skills. One way is to study books written by experts in your profession. But I've found that there is no better way to figure out what to teach than by going to a mentor, someone with years of knowledge and experience in your discipline. The really good ones know things inside and out, and I've found them to be easy to find, very accessible, and more than willing to share all they know. There is no better knowledge source than the voice of experience.

One word of caution here: Be careful not to make the list of basic skills too long. If you try to teach every basic skill under the sun all at once, you and the kids are in for frustration and failure. You'll have lots of possible skills to choose from, but avoid throwing too many at youngsters. Select the skills you deem most important (again, a mentor can help you here if you get stuck), then build on from there. When choosing skills, always take into consideration the mental, emotional, and physical abilities and limitations of your kids, along with the amount of time you have to teach these skills. It's important to be realistic in both these areas. You want to make sure you have enough time to do quality teaching while also keeping the skills within the ability range of your students or athletes.

- **DEVELOP A PLAN.** Use specific drills or lessons that will help young people learn the fundamental skills you've identified. You can find excellent examples in books and other reading materials in your discipline, but there's nothing like seeing it live in action. I would suggest watching how a mentor goes about teaching or coaching, and trying to adapt what he or she has found to be effective and worthwhile. Take notes on the drills and lessons used, then tailor them to match your learning setting and your kids' abilities. Finally, write it all down. Make an organized, specific plan that details everything you're going to teach and do in the amount of time you have with kids.

■ **COMMIT TO "REPPING THE FUNDAMENTALS."**
Sometimes it's boring to repeat the same drills and lessons over and over. But this is what it takes to build a strong learning foundation. So, commit to putting your plan into action with the understanding that you'll spend lots of time "repping the fundamentals," especially when you first start working with kids or work with kids who are new to your learning setting. Then, be patient! Give young people the time they need to learn and master the fundamentals. Eventually, you'll be able to move on to the more complicated material, but it takes time. Remember: Begin with the fundamentals and commit to working on them for as long as it takes youngsters to master them. Avoid the temptation to move on too quickly. Slow, steady progress almost always yields the best results.

■ **EVALUATE.** Take time periodically to assess how your kids are performing. Ask yourself questions like, "Do the kids understand what I'm trying to teach them?" and "Can they successfully do what I'm teaching them or are they struggling?" If your youth are confused or aren't meeting your performance standards, then modify your teaching to match their learning pace. For example, when my coaches and I watch a game film, we might determine that our defensive players are missing a lot of tackles. So, we adjust by increasing the amount of practice time we spend on the fundamentals of tackling. We'll do bread and butter drills that are specific to tackling over and over until it improves.

Huddle Up!

All coaches, teachers, and mentors need to focus on building solid foundations through teaching basic skills and "repping the fundamentals." This learning formula gives young people their best shot at improving and being successful. So, start at the beginning with the basics and stay there – don't leave until your kids really get it and are ready to move on.

Sometimes, "repping the fundamentals" can get old and stale. Don't allow this to happen! It's your job to bring energy and enthusiasm to your setting. When you bring that "get-up-and-go" attitude to your learning environment, it's quickly passed on to the kids. Get creative with drills and lessons, and make your learning environment a place that's fun, upbeat, and positive!

BUILDING A BETTER MOUSETRAP
Strategy: Seek Improvement

"My motto was always to keep swinging.
 Whether I was in a slump or feeling badly
 or having trouble off the field, the only thing
 to do was keep swinging."

– HANK AARON
Hit 755 Major League home runs

A t the end of every football season, I do a "self-
scout." This is a process where I pore over and
examine every nook and cranny of the football
program. Nothing is out-of-bounds or off-limits.
I look at player performance, coaching, practice

plans, game plans, play-calling, schemes, game decisions, game adjustments, off-season conditioning, and much more. All parts of the program – both in and off – are open to scrutiny. During the self-scout, I identify what's working well and what's not working well. I write down everything and make decisions about each area I've evaluated. I determine whether something is fine as it is, needs tweaking, needs a major overhaul, or needs to be completely scrapped and redesigned. This process takes time and a commitment to an open and honest approach. The goal is to look for ways to improve, no matter how small the change might be.

Every good coach who runs a successful program does some kind of thorough evaluation of his or her program at season's end. Some years bring minor adjustments, while others call for wholesale changes. The bottom line in all this is that change – big or small – is an integral part of improvement. I've never been fond of the motto, "If it ain't broke, don't fix it." Instead, I've got one that works better for me: "Look for ways to build a better mousetrap." This means you never stand still and are constantly on the lookout for ways to get better, even if it's just making minor or simple adjustments to things that have worked well in the past. Any change we make to our program is done in the spirit of progress and with the mindset of striving to improve and move forward.

The past few football seasons have been some of the best ever in Cowboy history – certainly during my tenure. But even when we've had a successful year, we never skip the self-scout process. And we find plenty of areas where we can adjust and make changes to help us get even better. For example, I've changed how we run our offense, how we stretch in practice and before games, how players can maintain and gain energy during halftime by eating the proper foods, how players acknowledge coaches during practice, how coaches can better use their time, how we can improve in our kicking game, and how we motivate players before games. People might think I'm crazy to mess with a good thing, especially after such a successful run. But in order to continue our success, I've got to look for ways to "build a better mousetrap" – and that involves change. My goal is keep our football program marching toward achievement and success, and that can't be done by standing still!

■ ■ ■

When I speak to teachers and coaches, I tell them that one of the best things that could happen to them and their kids is for all the file folders sitting in their cabinets and desk drawers to be destroyed. At first, most people just stare at me like I'm completely nuts. After all, this is the information they've relied on for years to decide how and what to teach, and how they should go about running their learning environment.

But my point in making this statement is that, over the years, anyone can become too dependent on the same old stuff. You stop looking for ways to update content and finding better ways to teach it. Such complacency can lead to "tired" lesson and practice plans that are outdated and worn out. Eventually, the learning environment grows stagnant and apathy settles in. The result is usually poor learning for the kids and burnout for the adults.

If all your file folders were destroyed, you would be forced to do a self-scout – and perhaps an extreme makeover – to find and implement new ways to go about teaching. It would give you the opportunity to research and discover innovative, exciting, and cutting-edge materials and techniques. This would help invigorate and add a freshness to your learning environment that would benefit both you and the youngsters you teach.

Change is a scary proposition; there's comfort in the familiar. But when done in a thoughtful and systematic manner, change also can be very positive and uplifting. Change for the sake of change is plain foolish and can bring on unnecessary risks. Instead, the focus and goal behind change should be to find new ways to become better at what you do and how you go about doing it. This way, your learning environment can remain a productive and effective place for kids to learn and succeed.

Push the Pile Forward

To build a better mousetrap in your learning setting, you have to maximize your talents and knowledge. This means being open to new ways of doing things. It also requires a willingness to put forth real effort – both time and energy – that's focused on uncovering new approaches. Working to improve your skills and knowledge is a big part of what it takes to do your job better and help kids succeed.

All people have natural skills and abilities that allow them to do some things a bit easier or a bit better than others. People also have other areas in their jobs and lives that they struggle with, difficulties that can prevent them from getting the most out of themselves. Some teachers and coaches are great motivators. It's easy for them to get young people excited about learning. But these same adults might struggle with organization and developing effective, quality lesson or practice plans that work well with kids in their setting.

Sometimes there are plays in a football game when the ball carrier gets caught in the middle of the swarm of tacklers and blockers. He hasn't been tackled yet, but he's been momentarily stopped. We teach our blockers and ball carriers to keep driving their feet, to keep "pushing the pile forward" so we gain that extra yard or two.

To become really good (and successful) at what you do, you have to focus on your weak areas and commit to improving them, while also continuing to look for ways to get better at the things you naturally do well. This focus and commitment is what separates the poor from the good and the good from the great. You can't control many parts of life, like the skills and abilities you were born with. But you can control your effort.

When you stop "pushing the pile forward," you're simply standing still. Eventually, you'll slide backward into mediocrity, and when this happens, failure is right around the corner. It's like being stranded in the ocean and deciding to tread water instead of heading for shore.

If you tread water, you'll stay afloat for a while, but eventually you're going to sink and drown. It's all wasted energy that gets you nowhere. Excellence requires resolve and putting forth the necessary blood, sweat, and tears needed to keep moving forward toward success. Your goal should be to keep your learning environment a fertile place for kids to learn. And you can do this only by constantly striving to find ways to improve yourself both personally and professionally.

A commitment to improving by giving it your all can pay off in many benefits to you, your youth, and your learning environment. Here are just a few:

- Youngsters have a better chance to learn and succeed. When you look for better or more effective ways to teach content, you enhance your teaching, which positively influences kids' learning.

- You are more likely to avoid burnout. New ideas and methods keep you fresh and excited.

- You create a learning environment where young people are upbeat and excited about learning.

- Kids gain confidence in your ability and believe you can help them achieve their goals. They buy in to you and your teaching, which makes learning easier.

- Youth learn how to put forth maximum effort. When they observe you working hard to improve yourself and the learning setting, they'll work hard at improving, too.

- Kids learn that change and effort shouldn't be feared or avoided, but instead embraced as ways to help them achieve their goals.

- You can create life-long learners. When young people see your commitment and effort to learn and challenge yourself, they see what it takes for them to achieve both inside and outside your learning setting.

- Kids learn how to deal with the many "curveballs" that life throws at them. They are better prepared to handle adversity and learn to be more resilient.

All-State

There's a football saying we use with our players: "Hard work beats talent when talent doesn't work hard." There was no better example of this than Pat, a former Cowboy football player. Pat wasn't a physically gifted athlete. He was undersized for a lineman and played against opponents much bigger than him every game. But Pat outworked everyone in the weight room and on the field. He made himself into a varsity football player by getting stronger lifting weights and hustling on the field all the way to the final whistle. His senior year, Pat was our most versatile lineman. Due to various injuries to other linemen during the season, Pat played just about every position on the offensive and defensive lines.

Weight training is an important part of becoming a successful football player. There are some kids on my team who are naturally bigger and stronger than others. But year after year, I see players like Pat with lesser physical gifts meet and exceed their potential by outworking many of those naturally stronger players. One way we help kids achieve in the weight room is to have them evaluate their daily performance and effort.

Anytime our players weight train, they self-rate their effort. We post a specific, detailed list that describes to kids what great effort looks like. For example, players can rate themselves an "A" effort and earn the tag "All-State" when they meet all of these requirements during their weight training session: sweat is pouring down their face, they complete all their lifts, and they encourage teammates to lift with maximum effort. Anything less than meeting the full criteria is rated a "B" effort with the label of "Average Joe." Not meeting any of the criteria leads to a "C" effort with the label of "Great Pretender."

We want all our players to be able to self-rate themselves as "All-State." On our team, players dislike the label "Average Joe," and they despise being called a "Great Pretender." Most times, what kids think is hard work and great effort isn't even close to what's expected. By giving them specific criteria for self-rating their effort, we help set them up to achieve their goals.

You can do the same thing in your learning setting by talking with youngsters about your expectations regarding their effort. Be specific; list and display the behaviors that demonstrate the effort you want to see. In addition, you can show them what hard work looks like through your own actions. Young people need to know exactly what you want from them.

When you model effort, it doesn't go unnoticed by kids. During the football season, I come to the football offices early on Sunday afternoons. It's a quiet time when I can sit down and develop game plans. During the following week, players will tell me they saw my vehicle parked in front of the building over the weekend. They see I'm working overtime to help make them and the team better, and it leads a lot of players to give a better effort. Remember: Never assume kids know how to work hard. Only through teaching and modeling do they learn what it really means and takes to be "All-State."

Never Satisfied

Many young people think that "being satisfied" is the same as "being content." I believe there is a difference between the two. To me, being content means you appreciate all you've got, while being satisfied means you're "okay" with where you're at. When you're satisfied, you're treading water and there's no movement forward.

One thing my players can never say once they're done playing football for me is that I didn't work hard to get the very best out of them and the team. One of my goals as a teacher and coach is to help kids learn not to be satisfied with just being "good enough." I want them to strive to be the best they can be at whatever they do, and to always be on the lookout for ways to improve.

This way, when adversity strikes in their lives (and it will!), they'll have the proper mindset and tools to meet it head on.

Effort and results don't always match up. Sometimes, youngsters can put forth great effort and achieve average results. For example, I've got students who work really hard in the classroom but aren't capable of earning better than C's or B's. I also have students who slack off, but can easily earn A's.

I'll take a classroom full of those hard-working students who earn average grades any day! I'm all about effort. Don't get me wrong; results do matter. But hard work and effort are what sets successful people apart from those who don't achieve goals. At some point in their lives, those "A" students who aren't really trying are going to run into situations where their natural abilities don't cut it anymore. If they haven't been taught to strive for more and give maximum effort, then they are in for frustration and failure.

My first Cowboy football team is a good example of this. In half our games that season, we had more talented athletes on the field than our opponents. We were bigger, stronger, and faster. But we only managed to win one game. Why? The players didn't understand how to give maximum effort or how to persevere through adversity.

Improving and striving for excellence are important life skills for young people to learn, no matter what their ability level is. These skills help set up kids for success both now and in the future. As teachers, coaches, and mentors, we are ultimately trying to help mold people to become the best parents, workers, friends, and citizens they can be.

A Winning Game Plan

It's important to develop the outlook that no matter how long you've been doing something, you can always get better. Many teachers and coaches leave their professions because they get burned out. This can happen for many reasons, but the biggest one might be that they've failed to seek new opportunities to grow though learning and change.

People can settle into a comfortable routine and rely on it for years and years. Many times, fear of the unknown keeps people from trying new things. Or, maybe they just lack the motivation and energy to seek out new and better ways of doing the job at hand. Whatever the reason, it's important for you to view change as a good thing and to put in the time and energy required to improve. Doing these things will help keep you fresh and on top of your game.

The following suggestions and ideas can help you stay on the learning track and feel more comfortable with discovering and introducing new ideas and methods into your learning environment.

- **DO A "SELF-SCOUT."** Look at all areas that affect your learning environment. This involves everything from your personal interactions with youth to the specifics of how you run your classroom and teach content. Leave no stone unturned. Evaluate each area and determine what's going well and what's not going as well as you would like. Next, decide what needs to be done in each area you've identified. Perhaps all that's needed are some minor adjustments. Or, you may need a complete overhaul. The important thing is to be open to any kind of change – big or small – that makes a particular area better.

The result of this kind of thorough self-analysis is positive and meaningful change. Stepping outside your comfort zone isn't easy, and it takes courage to do it. But without change, you run the risk of growing stale and dissatisfied in your job. When doing a self-scout, it's absolutely necessary to be honest with yourself. In fact, this is one of the most important things you can do during the process. To help with this, run your evaluations by others in your discipline who know you and your field well. This provides validation that you're on the right track as far as what's wrong (and right!), and gives you another point of view on what measures you should take. Don't be afraid to seek feedback and advice from others. My assistant coaches are a big part of my self-scout; let the people you respect and have faith in, and who know you and your learning environment well, be part of yours, too.

- **ATTACK YOUR RESOURCES.** Read books, attend clinics and seminars, observe and talk to mentors, and create opportunities to share ideas with others in your discipline. These are just a few good ways that you can gather information on what's new in your field. A willingness to gather ideas and seek new information, and then follow through on them, are what separates the great teachers and coaches from the average ones.

I've found that the best place to start is with mentors, those in your field who have years of experience to share with you. Look for people who are still excited about what they do and who aren't afraid to change how they do things. These people can offer a wealth of information and can make your learning journey easier.

One year, when I changed our offense because of the personnel I had coming back, I called a coach who had been successfully running this particular type of offense for years. He was more than happy to share with me what he knew and what he'd learned over the years. He even invited me over to his school and had some of his players demonstrate the formations and plays so I could get a better idea of how it all worked. He was gracious with his time and knowledge. Mentors know what works and what doesn't work with students and athletes because they've already trudged the road of trial and error. Talk to them about what clinics and seminars are worth attending, what materials are worth reading, what drills and lessons work well with kids, and any other tricks of the trade they've learned that you can benefit from.

■ **IMPLEMENT.** After you've determined what needs to be changed and how you can change it, incorporate the changes into your daily routine. Put together new lesson and practice plans that bring your new ideas and methods to life. This is where hard work comes in. It takes time and effort to redesign how you do things and to make it all fit in the time you have allotted. You can do a great self-scout and attack all your resources, but it means nothing unless you follow through and make it part of your learning setting. Transition takes time and flexibility, so allow yourself and your kids plenty of both to adjust to the changes. Also know that you'll always be "fine tuning" along the way.

Huddle Up!

A self-assessment process like a "self-scout" forces you to adjust, modify, and sometimes even completely remodel how you do things. But it enables you to get better at what you do and how you do it. Ultimately, the goal of change is to "build a better mousetrap," which means constantly striving for improvement. This keeps your teaching fresh and your kids excited about learning.

When you put in the effort to look for ways to get better, it's important to be honest in assessing your strengths and weaknesses. This can be tough! It's difficult for us to admit we're not as strong as we'd like to be in certain areas of our lives. Why? Because that means acknowledging that change is necessary. However, when you get past this, you'll be on the road to creating a learning environment where you are challenged and happy and where your girls and boys are getting the best you have to offer.

CHAPTER

HEROES NOT ZEROS
Strategy: Use Role Models

"I think it's an honor to be a role model to one person or maybe more than that. If you are given a chance to be a role model, I think you should always take it because you can influence a person's life in a positive light, and that's what I want to do. That's what it's all about."

– TIGER WOODS
Youngest golfer, at age 30, to reach 50 PGA career wins; second only to Jack Nicklaus in major championship victories

---

T o prepare my players for games, I try to moti-vate and inspire them by telling stories about real-life heroes. A few years ago, we had a very important game where I thought the two teams were evenly matched. Both were executing and playing at high levels. I firmly believed the outcome would come down to the intangibles of who was more resilient and showed the greatest heart. The winner was likely to be the one who wanted it most! For this particular game, we would need maximum effort and a strong desire to never give up.

After some research, I found the perfect example of a real-life athlete who had a story that demonstrated these qualities and someone the kids could relate to: Walter Payton, a former running back for the Chicago Bears. Payton played 13 seasons in the NFL and missed only one game – and that was in his rookie year. This was an amazing feat for a running back who was famous for taking and giving out tremendous hits. Payton won a Super Bowl title with the Bears and ended his career as the NFL's leading career rusher with more than 16,000 yards. Tragically, he died of a rare liver disease at age 45. Considered one of the greatest football players in history, Payton is also remembered for his outstanding personal qualities.

Early in the week before our game, I showed my players a film that documented Payton's humble beginnings growing up in poverty in rural Mississippi, his record-setting performances at Jackson State College, his stardom with the Bears in the NFL, and his bravery while facing certain death at a young age. Throughout the week, I also shared excerpts from his autobiography, "Never Die Easy," that spoke to the very qualities I wanted to instill in my players: toughness, courage, and heart. "Sweetness" (Payton's nickname) displayed all these qualities, both on and off the field in many different ways. I also developed a phrase that became our mantra for the week: play with a "Payton heart."

I took a chance and e-mailed the Walter Payton Foundation. The e-mail was addressed to Connie Payton, Walter Payton's wife, who is heavily involved in the Foundation's mission of providing help to neglected, abused, and underprivileged children. She quickly responded with a lengthy e-mail that talked about how her husband would have been very proud to be held up as a role model for the Cowboy players. She also included many other encouraging, uplifting, and motivational messages that I read to my players.

During my talk to the team just before kickoff, I spoke about all we had learned that week from Walter Payton's life and again challenged the players to play with a "Payton heart." I noticed that many of the players had written "Payton heart" or "34" (Payton's jersey number) on the athletic tape wrapped around their wrists, arms, and ankles. This was something they had done completely on their own. When I saw this, I knew the players had responded positively to Walter Payton's example and were inspired to play with character and determination. As expected, the game was close and hard-fought. In the end, we came out victorious. My guys played well and competed with "Payton hearts."

■ ■ ■

Role models can have a tremendous influence on young people. There's no doubt that Walter Payton's life story had a positive impact on my players and was a big factor in their effort and, ultimately, the game's outcome. Real-life examples of how others have faced and overcome tough situations with courage and character show kids that it can be done, even under circumstances more trying than their own. However, I believe the most important role models are the people who are closest to the youth and who interact with them every day.

You are a role model. Yes, you! As a matter of fact, all adults are role model candidates for kids. They look to us for guidance and direction, and they watch and emulate what we say and do. That's why it's our responsibility to use the right words and take the right actions when we are around kids, and even when we're not, because true character is revealed when others aren't watching. Girls and boys need real people like you to show them what it takes to live an honest, productive, and successful life.

Parents, older siblings, relatives, teachers, coaches, mentors, and others can have tremendous influence because they have direct contact and an intimate relationship with kids that famous people don't have. After all, how many youngsters are able to call up Tiger Woods and ask him how to handle a problem? The adults who are an integral part of kids' lives have the greatest opportunity to reach out and make an impact through their everyday teaching and example.

Story Power

Young people love stories. And I've found storytelling to be an excellent teaching and motivational tool. Telling stories is a great way to reinforce what you're teaching. That's why I'm always on the lookout for compelling stories that I can share with my students and players, especially ones that inspire and speak to how others have triumphed over adversity.

One story I like to share with students and athletes is about Erik Weihenmayer. He's climbed the "Seven Summits" (the tallest mountain on each of the seven continents), which include Mount Everest. When I tell his incredible story, kids intently listen to how this man's courage, determination, and tenacity enabled him to conquer the many challenges posed by climbing the loftiest peaks in the world. At the end of the story, they are dumbfounded to learn that Erik Weihenmayer is blind.

Hearing how others reach and even exceed their potential is exciting, educational, and motivating. However, I also think it's important for youngsters to read and hear about potential that's wasted, about those who've had it all in the palms of their hands, only to throw it away. That's why I have a bulletin board in my football office where I post articles about top athletes who've blown great opportunities by making poor choices and decisions about alcohol, drugs, grades, gangs, violence, and an assortment of other issues. Kids need to see that success isn't just about natural talent (intellectual ability or physical prowess) or luck; it's more about effort, determination, character, and what people choose to do with what they have.

Proven Winners

The content you teach from textbooks can be effective, but the message is even more powerful when students see it demonstrated through the lives and actions of others. Using role models and stories in your teaching helps make your job easier and learning more interesting and enjoyable for kids. There are many other benefits to using role models and real-life examples. Here are a few:

- They help motivate youngsters to continue working hard and striving toward success. Also, they are excellent teaching tools that can help kids who are struggling or are overwhelmed to stay on course and remain upbeat about learning.

- They reinforce your teaching and make it more credible. Real-life examples give the principles you're teaching (effort, determination, etc.) a "face" and a set of specific actions that show youth what to do.

- Kids learn how to go about handling similar situations in their own lives. The circumstances might not be as dramatic or exactly the same as the example you share, but there are usually common elements young people can relate to and solutions they can use with their own problems or issues.

- Role models give youngsters another voice of experience. Some kids get tired of hearing one voice all the time, and they might sometimes tune out what you're trying to teach. Telling others' stories provides you with new and fresh voices that grab their attention.

- Girls and boys hear about people doing the right things and succeeding. This helps them make the connection between what they do and what happens as a result. In other words, they learn that "right" actions are needed to achieve goals.

- Searching for good role model stories keeps your teaching fresh and current and helps you stay in tune with what appeals to young people.

- Role model stories show the differences between what it takes to succeed and what leads to failure. Stories can provide clear-cut examples of the right and wrong actions to take.

Young people need as many examples of real people doing the right things as you can give them. And, it's important for kids to know that the people around them contribute in quiet, positive ways to their home, school, neighborhood, and community. I firmly believe that the vast majority of adults are trying to live good lives and set good examples for young people, especially those adults who work with kids on a daily basis.

Today, people (kids especially) are fascinated with the lives of athletes, musicians, entertainers, and other celebrities. Television, magazines, and the Internet are overflowing with information about the rich and famous. Popular culture and the media report on almost every detail of celebrities' lives; in the process, how they live is glamorized, sensationalized, and held up as the example of what to strive for. This gives young people the message that fame, prestige, power over people, money, and possessions are the only ingredients that define and lead to success. This is not the message we want our kids to hear, or the values we want them to emulate, adopt, and work toward in their own lives.

This is why it's important for you to find and share with youngsters stories and examples of people – both famous and those in your own backyard – who are making positive contributions in whatever way they can, big or small. As teachers, coaches, and mentors, we need to be stabilizing forces in young people's lives. We have to constantly reinforce to them that positive values and pro-social behaviors like being kind and loving, helping others, and working hard are what really define and lead to success. So, do your homework and provide your young people with true and accurate examples of real people who have lived and succeeded in honorable ways marked by integrity and character.

Heroes Not Zeros

"Heroes Not Zeros" is an exercise I use in my classroom that can be incorporated into any learning setting. It helps youngsters to identify positive role models and gets them focused on how to achieve goals by taking the proper actions. The exercise is really very simple and can be an excellent addition to your teaching.

"Heroes Not Zeros" starts with awareness. Encourage youngsters (you can even make it an assignment) to look for examples of people who are succeeding and doing it the right way. You can make this exercise even more meaningful by having kids find stories within your discipline (education, sports, music, etc.) that address the specific principles (overcoming adversity, determination, etc.) you're teaching at the moment. For example, Walter Payton was the perfect role model example for me to use with my team because he was a football player and his story and life spoke to the very qualities (toughness, courage, and never giving up) I wanted to instill in my players.

Students can look for stories and examples in many places – books, magazines, newspapers, Web sites, TV, or the movies. Emphasize that stories can also come from their own family or their experiences or encounters with others who are close to them.

Once your kids have found examples, have them share them with others in your learning setting. A follow-up discussion is always beneficial and enhances teaching. Have youngsters identify the qualities that are displayed in each story and discuss how these qualities can be incorporated into their own lives or situations they might experience. This helps kids make the connection between the story and how it can apply to their own lives.

Once the first discussion is finished, have youngsters design a bulletin board where they can post all their inspirational and motivational stories. Label the bulletin board, "Heroes Not Zeros." For this exercise to be effective and have the greatest impact, do it often and, if possible, keep it going all through the year.

"Heroes Not Zeros" helps kids discover people who are living life the right way, using the very positive qualities you're teaching. It also shows them that the "heroes" of the world lead their good lives and do their good deeds both on a larger, more visible stage and in smaller, quieter everyday ways. The end result is that kids see that people in all walks of life are overcoming adverse circumstances and succeeding with character and dignity.

A Winning Game Plan

Role model stories are valuable and effective teaching tools; there's really no downside to using them. The good news is that these stories are fairly simple to incorporate into your teaching and can bring fun and excitement to your teaching.

Here are some suggestions and ideas for bringing role models to life in your learning setting.

- **KEEP YOUR ANTENNA UP.** Be on the lookout for examples of role models who embody the positive qualities (responsibility, persistence, courage, etc.) you'd like to teach kids. Keep your eyes and ears open as you read books, magazine articles, and newspaper stories, or surf the Web. Many TV shows, movies, and documentary films feature motivational stories and inspirational characters. Video is a medium that young people really like, and it provides an excellent change of pace from reading and lectures. I have a large video library that I draw from (movies like "Brian's Song," "Remember the Titians," "Stand and Deliver," "Mr. Holland's Opus," and many more) for situations or occasions where I want to highlight specific qualities.

It takes a little homework to find the role models you want to use with your kids. But once your antenna is up, you'll be surprised by how much material you'll find that can work. Alert others (spouses, friends, colleagues) to what you're doing. The more people who you have looking, the better; it helps to have more than one set of eyes and ears out there.

- **START A FILE.** Collect all the stories you gather and keep them organized for future use. Keep expanding your library. It's important to stay current with your role model examples, but history offers many great role models that stand the test of time and are still relevant with today's youngsters. There are wonderful stories throughout the ages of people who've lived amazing lives and overcome great obstacles. History's a great teacher, so be sure to use it!

Don't toss stories out unless they completely flop with kids. Remember that the young people you're currently working with will eventually be replaced by new faces. Save your examples and stories because it's easy to recycle them with the new youngsters.

■ **INCORPORATE STORIES INTO YOUR TEACHING.** Look for opportunities to use positive and inspirational stories and examples in your teaching and daily lesson plans. This takes time, effort, and preparation, but stories about good role models are great teaching tools for breaking up the monotony of the usual routine.

Before two-a-day football practices begin, I show my players a documentary film about kids who are locked up in a prison-like environment. These kids would trade places with my players in a heartbeat and gladly endure the rigors of two-a-day practices. This film has a much greater impact on my players than me lecturing them to be grateful for what they have and to work hard during this practice time. I've found that after watching this film, my players gripe less and look at what they have in a more positive light.

Most of the time, you'll have specific plans for when to use role model examples and stories. But remain open to using them spontaneously when situations arise in the world or in your own backyard. Take advantage of any opportunity to use role models in your teaching and learning setting.

■ **ENCOURAGE FURTHER EXPLORATION.** Almost every time I share a story with young people, someone wants to know more. Kids become intrigued and want to dig deeper. This is a golden opportunity to get them to read, research, and learn outside of your setting. When I presented Walter Payton's story to my players and read from his autobiography, several youth asked to borrow it so they could read the entire book. Some even went out and bought their own copy of the book. Connect kids to books and other materials that can help them further explore and expand their knowledge base. Take some time to get to know book titles, movies, Web sites, etc., so youngsters can follow up and learn more about what you've presented. With some kids, you may simply direct them to the library so they can do more research with a librarian's help. It's amazing what can happen when a kid's interest is piqued.

 Huddle Up!

True role models are those who possess great character and live by their principles. Role models are all around us at every level in life. They can give young people, especially those who are struggling, inspiration, strength, and hope. Encourage girls and boys to look for positive role models in the world around them. These examples help kids build their own positive roadmap for success.

CHAPTER

A CLASS ACT
Strategy: Build Character

"Be more concerned with your character than
with your reputation. Your character is what
you really are while your reputation is merely
what others think you are."

– JOHN WOODEN
Coached UCLA to 10 NCAA basketball titles

D uring the football off-season, I'm an assistant
coach for the Boys Town High School track
team. Track meets are usually very long sporting events. Many athletes participate and they're
all trying to keep their energy levels high with
plenty of foods and liquids. It's safe to say that
once a meet is over, a track venue is a pretty messy

183

place with wrappers, drink containers, athletic tape, and other garbage strewn about. That's why, at home and away meets, we have a team tradition: Our athletes pick up the trash not only in the area they occupied but also in the other teams' areas. And we don't leave until everything has been cleaned up.

A few years ago, as a meet was winding down, I handed out trash bags so our kids could get started on clean-up detail. This particular meet was an important, end-of-the-year event with lots of teams, athletes, and fans, so there was more garbage than usual. Once our kids finished in their area, they moved to the grandstands where the fans had been sitting all day. As we were cleaning up, several parents from other teams came up and told me what a great thing the kids were doing. One parent even joked that we not only won the meet but also picked up the trash afterwards! I explained to them it was all part of teaching our youth how to be good citizens, which is an important part of building good character. They were impressed with our kids and their actions, and commented that their teams and youngsters could benefit from doing the same thing.

A short time later, an announcement came over the public address system from the press box asking teams that had occupied the stadium's infield to pick up their area. Many coaches and athletes heard the announcement but just continued walking out of the stadium. They didn't bother to turn around and honor the request. Our boys immediately hustled down to the infield area and cleaned it up. Later, as we were leaving, the people in the press box came to our bus, thanked the guys, and gave them doughnuts for their effort and thoughtfulness.

■ ■ ■

Track meets are not the only place where our girls and boys "clean up." It's also tradition for our youth and fans to do the same thing after away football games. At first glance, this might appear to be just a nice gesture. But it is something really significant in the big picture of helping young people achieve their goals. Girls and Boys Town believes actions like this that teach respect and responsibility are vital to teaching kids how to succeed with character.

We all want the girls and boys we work with to do well and achieve, but it's important that they go about it the right way. This means learning and putting into practice the skills and traits that embody good character. Having kids do a simple task like picking up trash is a great opportunity for them to learn about citizenship, an important trait for good character development.

In your learning setting, your teaching reaches into many areas of kids' lives. Much of what you help youngsters learn involves the academic and behavior skills they need to succeed in school and in daily life once they leave school. But it's also important for you to teach the skills and traits that help shape character in individuals. This teaches young people how to achieve goals without taking shortcuts or steamrolling people.

It's possible for kids to achieve their goals without learning and using good character skills, but it usually ends up costing them in the long run (damaged relationships, loss of trust, etc.) with others. And while we all encourage our youth to work hard to achieve goals and find success, it should not be the end-all or sole focus in life. For kids to experience all the successes life has to offer, they must learn how to conduct themselves in honest, caring, and moral ways. When they make their journey with character, young people find that others are willing to stand up, cheer, and do all they can to help them succeed.

Character Really Does Matter!

Success in school, sports, or in other settings is great for kids, but only when it's done the right way, with integrity and honesty. Accomplishments pale when they're realized in dishonest and selfish ways. Character really does matter!

Girls and boys aren't born with the skills and traits that define and make up good character. Rather, they come into the world as self-centered creatures looking to get their needs and wants met in any way possible. As infants and toddlers, their behaviors and actions seem to say, "Me first!"

The good news is that all youngsters have the potential to grow into people of character. This is where you come in. Kids learn and develop character (and its skills and traits) over time from adults who are important in their lives. What you teach and how you behave can help young people learn how to go about achieving the right way. It's your duty to make sure the youth in your care have the opportunity to learn and exemplify the traits that make up positive character, including responsibility, honesty, empathy, respect, and fairness.

A lot of kids don't know what character means. I tell my players and students that character is determined by what people choose to do when no one is looking or would find out. This is a simple definition, but one that hits home with young people. It's easy to understand and immediately gets them thinking about what they would do in certain situations.

One year, I had been highlighting the character trait of caring with my football players. We talked in the classroom, in the locker room, and on the practice field about caring for each other and those close to us. The players knew my mother was battling cancer. Before a game later in the season, the team presented me with a bouquet of flowers to give to my mother. The kids had chipped in to pay for the flowers and they all signed a card wishing her well. They did all this on their own. It was then that I knew the lessons on caring had sunk in – and that was better than winning any game!

I also tell kids that character is an "all-the-time" thing. In other words, they can't turn it on and off when it suits them or to get what they want in certain situations. There will be many times when youngsters can either cut corners and take the easy route or stick to their guns and handle tough situations the right way. This is especially true when kids must decide not to follow the crowd when the crowd is involved in activities like underage drinking, drugs, sex, and cheating in school. Being a person of character isn't always easy to do, and no one does it perfectly all the time. But choosing to do the right thing because it's the right thing to do, despite what others might think, is what sets people of true character apart from the "wannabe's."

Training Ground

Sports and other extra-curricular activities provide excellent opportunities for teaching girls and boys lessons about character and reinforcing its skills and traits. Discussing and teaching topics like following rules, sportsmanship, and teamwork is one way to get the message across. You also see many opportunities to spontaneously reinforce and teach character almost every day. I often have players come to me after lifting weights to turn in valuable items like watches or wallets that others have left behind in the weight room. This is a great time for me to praise and reinforce the choices they made and actions they took that demonstrate positive character.

Most good and moral acts fall under one of the following general character traits outlined by "Character Counts!", a national character-building program: trustworthiness, respect, caring, citizenship, fairness, and responsibility. When you teach these skills and principles to kids by using the ideas and suggestions we've discussed in the previous 12 chapters, you're helping them learn what it means and takes to be a person of character.

As we've said, teaching character to young people is important for many reasons on many different levels. When a youngster develops and makes positive character traits part of his or her life, everyone – the youngster, the people around him or her, and others in society – benefits. Here are just a few of the many benefits of helping kids learn how to live lives of character:

- Reduced crime and delinquent activities

- Fewer unethical practices in school and business

- More functional families and homes

- Less drug and alcohol use and abuse

- Improved relationships within families and between schoolmates

- Better, more involved citizens of the community and the world

A Winning Game Plan

When our youth pick up trash following track meets and football games, we get many comments, phone calls, and letters complimenting them and their efforts. And we share all these accolades with the kids. This reinforces their behavior and helps them feel appreciated and good about what they're doing.

The goal for teachers, coaches, and mentors is to help youngsters turn positive character actions into habits or ways of life, not "sometime" behaviors they use only when it's convenient, easy, or gets them something they want. The following suggestions and ideas can help you incorporate character teaching into your learning setting.

■ **IDENTIFY CHARACTER SKILLS AND TRAITS.**
Determine what skills and traits you're able to focus on and teach. Much of this will be influenced by the nature of your discipline, your learning setting, and the amount of time you spend with kids. You won't be able to teach youth everything there is to know about character. So, figure out what skills and traits you feel comfortable teaching and which ones fit well into your learning setting. Choosing one or two character traits or skills is fine. Quality teaching on just one trait is better than no teaching at all or trying to cover everything in a limited time. Remember, keep it simple and focused. In football, we spend a lot time teaching the character trait of respect, which lends itself well to that setting. That means we model and teach how to respect our opponents, the officials, the fans, and the game. We do a lot of character teaching during summer conditioning, when we have more time. Every Friday for about an hour, all the coaches and players gather in a classroom to talk about a specific character trait. One of the coaches is assigned to define the trait to the players. Then, the coach gives examples of how to apply it in life and on the field. Then we answer questions from the players and stimulate

a group discussion. This process can work well in any setting, and kids seem to respond positively to the change of pace.

■ **PLAN AND IMPLEMENT.** Prepare lesson or practice plans that incorporate the traits and skills you decide to focus on. This takes time and effort. Thinking that you can simply squeeze or sprinkle in character teaching every now and then won't work. Your learning setting is a busy place and there's a lot to be accomplished in the short amount of time you have with kids. So, you have to carefully and meticulously plan your character teaching, just as you do with your content teaching. Write everything down and stick to your plan. Some adults think character teaching takes time away from content teaching. I've found that in the long run, it actually gives you more time to teach content because you've helped to create a more respectful environment where there is less negative behavior. When you teach a character trait like responsibility, youngsters begin to learn they have to take care of certain things like homework or other duties in the classroom on their own without being constantly told or reminded. All this helps to shape your setting into one that's conducive to learning.

Some teachers and coaches think character teaching and content teaching are separate and can't be mixed. This isn't true! It's fairly easy to weave character principles into the fabric of your teaching. A math teacher might decide to teach the character trait of honesty. He or she might spend some time talking about honesty and then have students practice it by occasionally correcting their own or another student's homework, quiz, or test. When you blend character teaching with content teaching, you can create a rich learning environment where your job is more satisfying and enjoyable and young people learn valuable life lessons.

■ **USE CONSEQUENCES.** When character issues arise, use consequences to reinforce behaviors and teach new ones. First, look for opportunities to use positive consequences to praise, reward, and reinforce positive character behaviors when youngsters use them. Catch kids being good when they display positive behaviors on their own, but also look for ways to encourage good character in kids.

At the end of each football season, we give out the "Competing with Character" Award. Even though it's our most prestigious award, and it usually goes to a player who isn't a superstar, the person who earns it is someone who puts the team first and is willing to do the little things – including the grunt work that others don't want to do – to help the team succeed.

When young people mess up and make mistakes, use negative consequences and teaching to help them learn alternative appropriate behaviors.

- **LEAD BY EXAMPLE.** Always be aware of your own behaviors – what you say and do. Modeling good character is one of the most effective and powerful ways to get your message across to youth. When you put your money where your mouth is and live a life of character, kids see that it is important and how it's done. During games, I model character by remaining calm through the adversity that comes with each game. Also, I always look to "work the problem" in a productive and composed manner. Doing this teaches my players to act and react in the same way when the heat is on during a game. Finally, no one is perfect, and that means adults too. When you mess up (and it will happen!) in front of the kids, take responsibility and make the situation right. There's no better way to teach young people how handle their mistakes than demonstrating it in a real-life situation. So, when something goes wrong and it's your fault, don't act like it didn't happen or simply let it hang out there unresolved. Move quickly to right the wrong or apologize and show kids how to handle tough situations the right way – with character!

Huddle Up!

What someone chooses to do when no one's looking is a good gauge of that person's character. Almost every day, kids come across new situations and people who test their commitment to living the right way. One slip up, one wrong decision at the wrong time, can have a dramatic and profound effect on the trajectory of a youngster's life – including derailing their chances to achieve their goals.

Teaching and reinforcing positive character traits and skills in your learning setting provides girls and boys with roadmaps for successfully navigating the potholes and detours that inevitably pop up in life. Ultimately, character teaching helps kids learn how to make good decisions and choices during good times and most importantly, in tough situations. As they grow into adulthood, they'll be armed with the character skills needed to live a life that benefits them and others.

COACH 'EM UP!

Most years, we have about 35 players on our Boys Town High School varsity football roster. Since we're a smaller high school, we encourage all the kids who are able and want to play football to participate. We simply need all the bodies we can get in order to have quality practices and a full and successful team. So, we end up with lots of youngsters who've never played before or who have very little experience with organized football.

Each season, only three to five kids on the squad have both the physical talent and internal motivation to become really outstanding players. Of the remaining 30 or so youth, some might have physical talent but lack motivation, while others might be motivated to play and get better but don't possess the physical tools needed to compete at a high level. This means that the majority of my players, year in and year out, are kids who either aren't athletically gifted or aren't always motivated to practice and play with great effort. Even so, every one of these players is very important to our team's success. If one of them isn't getting the job done and performing the way we need him to, we can't simply give him an F and send him on his way. Why? Because there isn't anyone to take his place! I tell my assistant coaches that the vast majority of our players need to be "coached up." By that, I mean that we not only must teach football skills but also must convince these kids that they are valued, that they are important persons and players, and that they can help the team succeed if they try their best. After all, three to five talented and motivated players can't succeed and win by themselves in a team game like football. They need a full complement of teammates around them who are willing and able to fill unglamorous but crucial roles if our team is to do well. How successful my coaches and I are in teaching, developing, and motivating the other 30 or so players is a major factor in what kind of season we have each year.

■ ■ ■

It's easy to teach and be successful with naturally gifted and internally driven youth who have a desire to achieve. Unfortunately, these kinds of kids are far more the exception than the rule in most learning settings.

Just like my football team, your setting may include many more youngsters who have some kind of deficit or limitation (intellectual, physical, mental, emotional, or motivational) that hinders their progress and ability to move forward. Your job and the challenge you face is to "coach 'em up!"

Skilled and dedicated teachers, coaches, and mentors are willing and able to go the extra mile to find and develop new ways of helping kids achieve, regardless of the obstacles in their lives. Let's face it, moving talented and motivated youth from point "A" to point "B" often requires little effort on your part. Most of these kids can do all the work on their own. Your main responsibility is simply to steer them and cheer them on.

The real work and challenges you face are with the girls and boys who struggle to achieve goals. These young people and their unique circumstances will take up the biggest chunk of your time and effort. This is where your skills and abilities as a teacher and motivator are put to the test, and where the real teaching battle is won or lost.

To help these kids learn and succeed, you have to arm yourself with the best teaching and motivational tools and techniques available. What works for one youngster won't necessarily work for other youth. There's usually a whole different set of dynamics going on from kid to kid that make issues or problems that appear to be similar very unique. For example, you might not know a youth is having problems with friends or at home or that she just broke up with her boyfriend. These types of issues undoubtedly have a direct impact on a kid and his or her ability and desire to learn and move forward. That's why it's imperative for you to get to know each one of your kids and their situations as best you can, to stay on top of the cutting-edge materials and teaching techniques in your discipline, and to be willing to add your own creative touches to making new things work for your setting and your kids.

Committing yourself to helping youngsters who are struggling – whether it's with content, behavior, motivation, or another issue – is what working with kids is all about. These are the youth who will pose the greatest challenges. But they'll also give you the greatest joy and sense of satisfaction when they do achieve. Experiencing success is new to most of these kids, and it's extra special for them (and you!) when it happens.

Meet the Challenge!

There are times when I hear teachers criticize their students over poor results on tests or quizzes. Often, teachers try to explain that poor performance is a result of students not "getting it" or not being "motivated." These explanations are sometimes just excuses for ineffective teaching.

One of your main responsibilities is to teach young people how to succeed despite the obstacles they face in their lives. Many kids simply don't have the skills or experience to do this by themselves yet. They need a professional guide like you to show them the right way to go around, over, or through their particular roadblocks. This kind of teaching is so vital because it can help alter, even completely change, the arc of a youngster's life – and it doesn't get any more important and special than that!

However, working with young people isn't always an easy task. One year, I had a player, Anthony, who exploded onto the high school football scene. When he came to Boys Town High School as a sophomore, he had never played a down of organized football before. He was big, fast, and instinctively understood how to play running back.

At the end of the season, Anthony had rushed for more than 1,600 yards and was selected as an all-state running back. He was raw and just learning how to play the position. His future was bright and the sky was the limit on the football field. Division I football coaches began recruiting Anthony, something that just doesn't happen with our players.

My assistant coaches and I had high hopes for the next season as we began developing our offense around Anthony's exceptional ability. We had the opportunity to be a very good football team. Before the season started, Anthony made several poor decisions and choices. He was given his fair share of second chances, but he ended up leaving Girls and Boys Town to return to a home environment that offered nothing but a dead end.

It was frustrating to lose a talented player like Anthony. We rarely get athletes of his caliber. Even more frustrating and disappointing was losing Anthony the student and human being. He had come a long way in school and with his behaviors; he was making progress. It was sad to see Anthony squander the opportunity to grow, learn, and succeed at Girls and Boys Town.

We all get our share of kids like Anthony. The ups and downs of working with kids like this can leave you uncertain and tentative. But in order to do the job right, you need to have confidence, patience, persistence, enthusiasm, and a desire and willingness to grow and change. To keep kids moving toward success, you have to be the leader, the one willing to shoulder the majority of the responsibility to help make it all happen. This doesn't mean you do the kids' work for them; it does mean that your kids know that they can count on you to show the way when they need help.

There will be days when you become frustrated and disappointed because youth aren't positively responding to you and your teaching. These are the times when many adults are tempted to throw it all back on the kids and blame the lack of progress and motivation on their limitations. During these rocky periods, it's important for you to remain composed and positive, and to remember that tough times, sticky problems, and large obstacles all come with the territory. They're inevitable and unavoidable. The key is to always stay solution-oriented and continue working hard to find new and innovative ways to keep young people interested in learning and moving down the right path.

So, What Are You Going to Do Now?

Okay, you've learned about some new ideas and ways to deal with kids and improve your learning setting. Now the question is: "What are you going to do with all this information?" Well, there are two options: Sit back and think about it or take action. It's a choice. Don't let apathy or the fear of trying something new govern the choices you make for your youngsters and learning setting. Be bold and courageous! In the end, both you and the kids will win – big time!

I've learned that the best time to strike is while the iron is hot, and that's right now, when you're filled with passion and willingness! So get started right away. Don't wait! Procrastination is a killer of great ideas.

Keep in mind that I'm not talking about wholesale changes here. I'm talking about sitting down and writing out a plan of action that you'd like to follow and some timelines for making it happen. The first step in making new ideas and changes a reality is careful planning. After that, follow up with action and execution. Also, share with your colleagues what you've learned and how you plan to use it. They'll help you shape your ideas into workable steps that fit your discipline and learning setting.

You don't have to use everything we've discussed in the book. Simply take what works for you and keep the rest in reserve. (It might come in handy someday.) You might only take one idea from this book or you might find several that are helpful and useful. Also, you might choose to adapt and refine a suggestion or idea so it works best to meet your needs. My point here is to encourage you to take what you've read and treat it like a piece of clay – play with it, shape it, mold it, and make it your own. A suggestion or an idea combined with an open mind and a willing spirit can bring forth incredible things!

You Are That Person

Think back to a person outside of your family who helped you achieve and move forward in life. Most people name a teacher, a coach, or another mentor. This person had a positive influence on you, stuck by your side during thick and thin, and taught you what it took to persevere and succeed.

Guess what? You can be that person for kids! You can single-handedly change the life of a youngster and get him or her pointed in the right direction!

Most times, you won't even be aware of the impact you're having on young people. The letter at the beginning of the book from one of my former football players is a great example of this. This particular youngster wasn't a star player or even one who played much in games. And he wouldn't have been on my short (or long!) list of players I've coached over the years whom I would expect to write that letter. He wasn't a youngster I thought I had influenced much before he graduated from Boys Town.

But his letter reminded me that we have tremendous power to change the course of kids' lives just by coming to work every day and doing the best job we can. Just because you can't see progress doesn't mean it's not happening. In many cases, you're planting seeds that might lie dormant for a long time before they spring to life. So don't take any days off! Always give your best effort and do whatever it takes to help each one of your kids move forward toward success.

Don't settle for the "same old, same old." Instead, be fearless and daring! Seek out innovative teaching techniques and new methods of working with youth. This kind of attitude, thinking, and action can keep you moving forward with eagerness and success. In the end, this is what will help kids the most. Your passion for learning and commitment to continued growth can be two of the greatest lessons you ever give your kids!

As Boys Town founder Father Edward Flanagan once said, "When you help a child today, you write the history of tomorrow."

CREDITS:

Editor:	Michael Sterba, M.H.D.
Book Cover and Layout:	Anne Hughes
Front Cover Photography:	Mike Buckley